Better Homes and Gardens®

OneDish Meals

© Copyright 1981 by Meredith Corporation, Des Moines, Iowa.
All Rights Reserved. Printed in the United States of America.
Large-Format Edition. Sixth Printing, 1986.
Library of Congress Catalog Card Number: 80-68451
ISBN: 0-696-01245-6

On the cover: Elegant enough for company, *Spinach Spaghetti Pie* features a rich and flavorful filling that includes spinach, pork sausage, cottage cheese, and cream cheese, all in a pasta crust (see recipe, page 20).

BETTER HOMES AND GARDENS® BOOKS

Editor: Gerald M. Knox
Art Director: Ernest Shelton

Food and Nutrition Editor: Doris Eby
Senior Food Editor: Sharyl Heiken
Senior Associate Food Editors:
Sandra Granseth, Elizabeth Woolever
Associate Food Editors: Bonnie Lasater,
Julia Martinusen, Diana McMillen,
Marcia Stanley, Diane Yanney
Recipe Development Editor: Marion Viall
Test Kitchen Director: Sharon Stilwell
Test Kitchen Home Economists:
Jean Brekke, Kay Cargill, Marilyn Cornelius,
Maryellyn Krantz, Marge Steenson

Associate Art Directors:
Neoma Alt West, Randall Yontz
Copy and Production Editors: David Kirchner,
Lamont Olson, David A. Walsh
Assistant Art Director: Harijs Priekulis
Senior Graphic Designer: Faith Berven
Graphic Designers: Alisann Dixon,
Linda Ford, Lynda Haupert, Lyne Neymeyer,
Tom Wegner

Editor in Chief: Neil Kuehnl
Group Editorial Services Director:
Duane Gregg
Executive Art Director: William J. Yates

General Manager: Fred Stines
Director of Publishing: Robert B. Nelson
Director of Retail Marketing: Jamie Martin
Director of Direct Marketing:
Arthur Heydendael

One-Dish Meals
Editor: Bonnie Lasater
Copy and Production Editor: David A. Walsh
Graphic Designer: Neoma Alt West
Consultant: Joyce Trollope

Contents

One Dish Meals

Not only casseroles, but also skillet meals, soups, stews, as well as sandwiches and salads are in this collection of one-dish meal recipes. Each recipe can serve as the meal's mainstay, be it light brunch or substantial dinner meal. For most, a salad, dessert, beverage, and perhaps bread or rolls are all that's needed to make the meal complete. Variety and versatility abound in this tempting selection ranging from family fare to elegant one-dish meals for entertaining. Shown here are Hearty Pilaf Casserole (1), Peanut-Chicken Salad (2), Cornish Beef Pasties (3), Oriental-Style Pork Steaks (4), Texas-Style Hot Chili (5), and Lamb-Spinach Pie (6) (see index for recipe pages).

CookwarePrimer

The cookware used to prepare one-dish meals is as varied and versatile as the recipes themselves. To help you in your recipe preparation, we've included the basics of choosing and using cookware for one-dish cookery. Although very specialized cookware is unnecessary in one-dish cookery, the cookware used is important because its size, shape, and material can affect a recipe. Shown on this and the next two pages are some of the cookware most suitable for making the recipes in this book. (Numbers on the diagrams correspond to the numbers of each utensil discussed here.) The **stock pot (1)** commonly is made of aluminum; has two handles; has tall, straight sides; and exposes only a small surface area of the simmering liquid, which reduces evaporation. A Dutch oven or large saucepan can be substituted for a stock pot. The **soufflé dish (2)** traditionally is made of white ovenproof porcelain and has straight sides and a flat bottom. The outside may have ridges. Its classic use is for preparing soufflés, although it can be used also for a variety of refrigerator and oven-to-table foods. The straight sides allow a soufflé to "climb" and have more height than a deep casserole does. The **saucepan (3)** is a basic piece of cookware and comes in many styles and materials. It should have a flat bottom, straight sides that usually curve into the bottom, and one long handle. It also may have a pouring lip and a cover. Saucepans are used for cooking and heating liquid mixtures. The **electric skillet (4)** is available in both square and round shapes and has a built-in heating element with a thermostatic control. The heating control unit may be detachable to make the skillet immersible in water. Covers for electric skillets may be vented to allow steam to escape during cooking. Domed covers are available to accommodate large cuts of mat or poultry. Follow the manufacturer's directions for adapting recipes to its use.

Skillets (5) come in a variety of sizes and materials or combination of materials: aluminum, stainless steel, rolled or carbon steel, cast iron (also enameled cast iron), porcelain-enamelware, heat-resistant glass, and copper. Cast-iron skillets require conditioning, as do some made of aluminum or an alloy of aluminum. (See page 31 for seasoning instructions.) Skillets may have a "non-stick" coating on the inside surface. A skillet is usually round and shallow with a flat, wide bottom, and one handle. Its low sides can be vertical, sloped, or even flared as in an omelet pan, a variation of the skillet. Most commonly used for baking main-dish and dessert pies, the **pie plate (6)** is a round open dish with low flared sides. It is made of glass, ceramic, or Pyroceram. Also available are pie pans made of aluminum, tin, and enameled steel. Some pie pans have a depressed rim to prevent the filling from running over the edge. The **wok (7),** Chinese in origin, is used for "stir-frying," a cooking method in which small pieces of food are constantly stirred while cooking quickly over high heat. Woks also can be used for steaming foods. A rack-type insert placed inside the wok holds the food above boiling liquid, and a cover holds in the steam. Woks have a wide rounded bottom, sloping sides, one or more handles, and a cover. They are usually made of aluminum or rolled steel. Long-handled, shovel-shaped utensils are used for stirring the food. A ring stand, placed wide end *down*, is used to hold the wok above a gas flame.

For electric ranges, place the wide end of the ring stand *up* over the largest heating element. A new wok should be seasoned before using (see page 87 for instructions). A large skillet can substitute for a wok. The **clay baker (8),** made of unglazed clay, is a covered, usually oval-shaped vessel, with ridges on the inside bottom that hold the food above the cooking juices. When soaked in water before using, the utensil absorbs moisture released during baking. To prevent cracking the clay baker, sudden temperature changes should be avoided when using it; so place it in a cold oven, rather than a preheated one. Also, any warm or hot liquids should be added only after the baker and its cool contents have warmed. When removing a clay baker from the oven place it on a folded cloth or wooden board. The **covered roasting pan (9)** is usually used for roasting poultry or large cuts of meat, but also can be used to prepare large-quantity casseroles. It is oblong, round, or rectangular, and commonly made of aluminum, porcelain-enamelware, cast iron, or enameled cast iron. Some have a rack or perforated tray to hold the contents off the pan's bottom.

The **quiche dish (10)** originated in France and is similar to a pie plate's shape, except the quiche dish has straight, fluted sides. It is usually used for making quiche, a custard pie made with cheese. Ceramic quiche dishes are available, as well as metal ones, which have a removable bottom. A pie plate can also be used to bake a quiche. The **Dutch oven (11),** which dates to colonial days, is a large, deep, round pan with a tight-fitting domed cover. It has two handles and may be used on the range-top as well as in the oven. Only recently has it been made of materials other than cast iron. Today Dutch ovens are also made of heavy-gauge aluminum, stainless steel, and enameled cast iron. **Casseroles (12)** are oval or round baking dishes, with or without handles, and usually with a cover. They are generally made of heatproof glass, ceramic, Pyroceram, porcelain, or china. Casseroles are usually used for baking mixtures by the same name and for a variety of other foods. **Baking dishes (13)** are shallow, with a rectangular or square shape, and come in a variety of sizes. They are made of heatproof glass, Pyroceram, china, porcelain, and earthenware. Baking

pans come in similar shapes and sizes as baking dishes and are made of aluminum, stainless steel, copper, and enameled cast iron. Neither baking dishes nor baking pans come with lids. Because it is shallow, food cooked in a baking dish will cook more quickly than in a casserole. The **electric slow crockery cooker (14)** is designed for long cooking periods. The crockery cooker simmers food at low heat for several hours (8 to 10 usually). The heating element wraps around the sides or bottom of the crockery liner. Or, is some cases the heating unit, similar to a small hot plate, is separate from the vessel. (All crockery cooking recipes in this book were tested, using only the former type.) These have very low wattage and the element is on continuously. All crockery cookers come equipped with a cover. The cover should not be lifted during the cooking time since this causes heat loss and increases the cooking time. Sudden temperature changes should be avoided, so cold foods or liquids should not be added to a hot cooker.

One Dish Meals

Casseroles & Skillet Meals

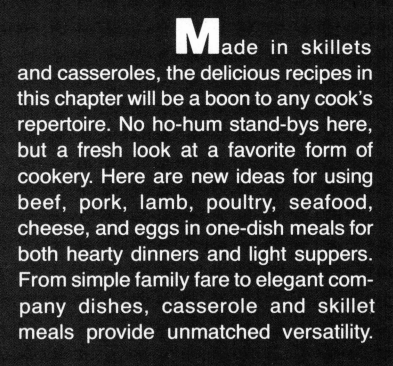

Made in skillets and casseroles, the delicious recipes in this chapter will be a boon to any cook's repertoire. No ho-hum stand-bys here, but a fresh look at a favorite form of cookery. Here are new ideas for using beef, pork, lamb, poultry, seafood, cheese, and eggs in one-dish meals for both hearty dinners and light suppers. From simple family fare to elegant company dishes, casserole and skillet meals provide unmatched versatility.

Create·a·Casserole

Meat and Pasta Bake

4 ounces pasta
1½ pounds ground meat
1 cup thinly sliced celery
½ cup chopped onion
1 10¾-ounce can condensed soup
1 cup shredded cheese (4 ounces)
½ cup liquid
1 teaspoon Worcestershire sauce
¾ teaspoon dried seasoning, crushed
¼ teaspoon salt
¼ cup fine dry bread crumbs
1 tablespoon melted butter *or* margarine

Cook pasta according to package directions; drain and set aside. In a 12-inch skillet cook meat, celery, and onion till meat is browned and onion is tender. Drain off excess fat. Stir in desired soup, cheese, liquid, Worcestershire, seasoning, salt, and pasta. Turn into a 2-quart casserole. Stir together bread crumbs and melted butter or margarine; sprinkle atop. Bake in 350° oven for 45 minutes or till heated through. Makes 6 servings.

Pasta Options
spaghetti
medium egg noodles
elbow macaroni

Meat Options
beef, pork,
or lamb

Soup Options
cream of onion
cream of chicken
cream of potato

Liquid Options
beef broth
chicken broth
apple juice

Cheese Options
American
cheddar
Monterey Jack

Seasoning Options
thyme
marjoram
savory

Create·a·Skillet/Meal

Meat and Vegetable Skillet

1 pound ground meat
¼ cup chopped onion
¼ cup chopped green pepper
1 10¾-ounce can condensed soup
½ cup milk
½ teaspoon dried thyme, crushed
½ teaspoon dried basil, crushed
¼ teaspoon salt
2 cups starch option
1 10-ounce package frozen vegetable
   Croutons *or* canned French-fried onions
   (optional)

In a 10-inch skillet combine meat, onion, and green pepper. Cook till meat is browned and onion is tender; drain off excess fat. Combine soup, milk, thyme, basil, and salt. Stir into meat. Add starch option and desired vegetable. Cover; simmer 25 to 30 minutes or till heated through, stirring occasionally. If desired, garnish with croutons or French-fried onions. Serves 4.

Meat Options
beef, pork, or lamb

Soup Options
golden mushroom
cream of celery
cream of chicken

Vegetable Options
mixed vegetables
cut green beans
whole kernel corn

Starch Options
- frozen loose-pack hash brown potatoes, partially thawed
- cooked rice
- cooked barley

Veal and Wild Rice Casserole

2¾ cups water
1 cup wild rice, rinsed
1 tablespoon instant beef bouillon
    granules

1¼ pounds veal leg round steak, cut ½ inch
    thick
2 tablespoons cooking oil
2 cups sliced fresh mushrooms
1 small onion, sliced and separated into
    rings
½ teaspoon dried chervil, crushed
¼ teaspoon dried thyme, crushed
¼ teaspoon dried savory, crushed
⅓ cup dry white wine
½ cup dairy sour cream
1 tablespoon all-purpose flour
    Paprika

In medium saucepan combine water, wild rice, and instant beef bouillon granules. Bring to boiling; reduce heat. Cook, covered, over low heat for 45 to 50 minutes or till water is absorbed. Meanwhile, cut veal steak into 5 serving-size pieces. Pound each piece with meat mallet to ¼-inch thickness. In large skillet brown veal pieces in hot cooking oil. Add sliced mushrooms and onion. Combine chervil, thyme, and savory; sprinkle over mushrooms and onion. Pour dry white wine over all. Cover and cook 5 minutes over medium heat. Remove from heat.

Turn cooked wild rice into a 12x7½x2-inch baking dish. Arrange veal pieces on top of the wild rice. Using a slotted spoon, remove mushrooms and onions from liquid in skillet and place atop veal. Measure drippings in skillet; add water if necessary to make ¾ cup liquid. Return liquid to skillet. Combine sour cream and flour; add to liquid in skillet. Cook, stirring constantly, till mixture is thickened and bubbly. Pour sour cream mixture over veal and vegetables in casserole; sprinkle with paprika. Bake, covered, in 325° oven for 20 minutes. Makes 5 servings.

Nacho Casserole

1 pound ground beef
½ cup chopped onion
1 16-ounce can pork and beans in tomato
    sauce
1 12-ounce can whole kernel corn with
    sweet peppers
1 10¾-ounce can condensed tomato soup
1½ to 2 teaspoons chili powder
1 4½-ounce package tortilla chips
1 4-ounce can green chili peppers, rinsed,
    seeded, and chopped
2 cups shredded Monterey Jack cheese
    (8 ounces)

In 10-inch skillet cook ground beef and onion till meat is browned and onion is tender. Drain off fat. Stir in pork and beans, corn, tomato soup, and chili powder. Turn into 12x7½x2-inch baking dish. Bake, covered, in 350° oven for 30 minutes. Remove from oven and arrange tortilla chips atop. Sprinkle with chopped chili peppers and shredded cheese. Return casserole to oven and bake, uncovered, 5 minutes more. Serve immediately. Makes 6 servings.

Choosing Ground Beef

When shopping for ground beef, look on the label for the phrase "Not Less Than X% Lean." For the best value, purchase ground beef with the percentage of lean best suited for your recipe.

Use ground beef that is 70-75 percent lean when your recipe calls for drippings to be poured off or removed.

When you want the meat to hold its shape and be juicy but not greasy, use 75-80 percent lean ground beef.

For low-calorie diets, use ground beef that is 80-85 percent lean. Remember, however, that this ground beef won't be very juicy unless you add other ingredients to provide moistness.

Mushroom-Zucchini Meat Pie

1 beaten egg
½ cup milk
½ cup seasoned fine dry bread crumbs
¼ teaspoon salt
  Dash pepper
1 pound ground beef

½ cup chopped onion
3 tablespoons dry red wine
1 cup sliced zucchini
1 4-ounce can mushroom stems and
  pieces, drained
1 8-ounce can pizza sauce
1 teaspoon prepared mustard
3 to 4 ounces American *or* cheddar
  cheese, sliced and quartered
  diagonally

In a mixing bowl combine egg, milk, bread crumbs, salt, and pepper. Add ground beef; mix well. Press meat mixture into bottom and onto sides of a 9-inch pie plate to form a shell. Bake in a 350° oven for 25 minutes. Drain off fat.

Meanwhile, in covered medium skillet cook chopped onion and dry red wine till onion is almost tender. Stir in sliced zucchini and mushrooms; cook, uncovered, 2 to 3 minutes more or till vegetables are tender. Stir in pizza sauce and prepared mustard; heat through.

Spoon vegetable mixture over baked meat shell; place cheese triangles atop. Return to 350° oven and bake 5 minutes more or till cheese melts. Makes 6 servings.

Microwave cooking directions: In medium nonmetal bowl combine onion, wine, zucchini, and mushrooms; cook, covered with waxed paper, in counter-top microwave oven on high power for 7 to 8 minutes or till vegetables are tender. Stir in pizza sauce and mustard; set aside. Prepare meat mixture as directed above. Press into nonmetal 9-inch pie plate to form a shell. Micro-cook, uncovered, for 8 minutes, giving dish a half-turn once. Drain off fat. Spoon vegetable mixture over meat shell; place cheese triangles atop. Micro-cook, covered, for 1 to 2 minutes or till cheese melts.

Chili Polenta Deep-Dish Pie

13

¾ cup yellow cornmeal
¾ cup cold water
¾ teaspoon salt
2 cups boiling water
1 15-ounce can *and* one 7½-ounce can
  chili with beans
1 16-ounce can red kidney beans, drained
¼ cup minced dried onion
1 teaspoon paprika
¼ teaspoon curry powder

Stir together cornmeal, the ¾ cup cold water, and salt; gradually add to the 2 cups boiling water, stirring constantly. Cook till thick, stirring frequently. Cover; cook over low heat 10 to 15 minutes. Cool slightly. Pour into a 1½-quart casserole, pushing up sides to form a shell. Cover surface with waxed paper; chill. Combine chili with beans, kidney beans, onion, paprika, and curry powder; spoon into cornmeal shell. Bake, covered, in 400° oven for 30 minutes; uncover and bake 10 to 15 minutes more or till heated through. Serves 4.

Hearty Pilaf Casserole

1 pound ground beef
¾ cup bulgur wheat
½ cup sliced green onion
¼ cup chopped green pepper
1 clove garlic, minced
1 16-ounce can tomatoes, cut up
1 pound zucchini, cut into ¼-inch slices
1 tablespoon Worcestershire sauce
1¼ teaspoons salt
1¼ teaspoons dried oregano, crushed
1 teaspoon sugar
  Dash bottled hot pepper sauce
1 cup shredded cheddar cheese
  (4 ounces)

In large skillet cook beef, uncooked bulgur wheat, onion, green pepper, and garlic till meat is browned and onion and pepper are tender. Drain. Stir in *undrained* tomatoes, zucchini, Worcestershire, salt, oregano, sugar, and pepper sauce. Turn into 2-quart casserole. Bake, covered, in 350° oven about 45 minutes. Sprinkle cheese atop. Serves 6.

Mexican Corn Bread Casserole

1 cup yellow cornmeal
½ teaspoon baking soda
½ teaspoon salt
1 cup milk
2 beaten eggs
1 17-ounce can cream-style corn
2 cups shredded cheddar cheese
1 4-ounce can green chili peppers, rinsed,
    seeded, and chopped
½ cup chopped onion
1 pound ground beef
1 16-ounce can red kidney beans, drained
½ of an 8-ounce can (½ cup) tomato sauce
2 teaspoons chili powder
¼ teaspoon garlic powder
    Yellow cornmeal

In a bowl stir together the 1 cup cornmeal, the baking soda, and the salt; stir in milk, eggs, and corn. Stir in cheese, chili peppers, and onion; mix till well blended.

Meanwhile, in a large skillet cook ground beef till browned; drain. Stir in kidney beans, tomato sauce, chili powder, and garlic powder; cook till heated through.

Grease and sprinkle a thin layer of cornmeal over the bottom of a 12x7½x2-inch baking dish. Turn *half* of the cornmeal batter into the dish. Cover with the meat-bean mixture and top with the remaining cornmeal batter. Bake in a 350° oven about 45 minutes or till topping is done. Serve immediately. If desired, garnish with hot cherry peppers and fresh cilantro. Makes 6 servings.

Beefy Bean and Rice Skillet

- 1 pound ground beef
- ½ cup chopped onion
- ½ cup sliced celery
- ½ cup chopped green pepper
- 1 16-ounce can tomatoes, cut up
- 1 16-ounce can red kidney beans
- 1 8-ounce can tomato sauce
- ¼ cup water
- 1½ teaspoons chili powder
- 1 cup quick-cooking rice
- ¾ cup shredded Monterey Jack cheese

In large skillet cook beef, onion, celery, and green pepper till meat is browned and vegetables are tender. Drain off fat. Stir in *undrained* tomatoes, *undrained* kidney beans, tomato sauce, water, chili powder, and 1 teaspoon *salt*. Bring to boiling; stir in rice. Cover and reduce heat. Simmer, stirring occasionally, 10 to 15 minutes or till rice is cooked. Sprinkle cheese atop; cook, covered, 1 minute more. Serves 6.

Beef-Spinach Casserole

- 1 pound ground beef
- 1 4-ounce can sliced mushrooms, drained
- 2 10-ounce packages frozen chopped spinach
- 1 cup dairy sour cream
- ½ cup shredded cheddar cheese
- ½ cup grated Parmesan cheese
- ¼ cup milk
- 2 tablespoons *regular* onion soup mix
- 1 cup plain *or* herb-seasoned croutons
- 3 tablespoons butter *or* margarine, melted

In a 10-inch skillet cook ground beef till meat is browned. Drain off fat. Stir in mushrooms. Cook spinach according to package directions; drain well, pressing out excess liquid. Combine sour cream, cheddar cheese, Parmesan cheese, milk, and dry soup mix. Stir into meat mixture along with drained spinach. Turn into a 10x6x2-inch baking dish. Bake, covered, in 350° oven for 20 minutes. Meanwhile, combine croutons and butter or margarine; mix well. Sprinkle atop casserole. Bake, uncovered, for 10 minutes more. Serves 5 or 6.

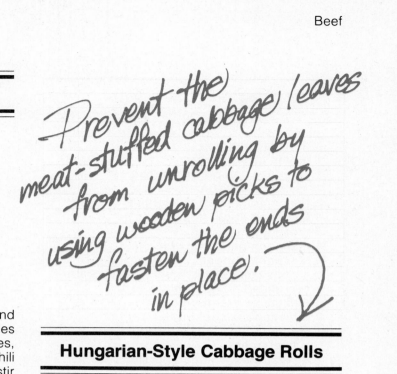

Prevent the meat-stuffed cabbage leaves from unrolling by using wooden picks to fasten the ends in place.

Hungarian-Style Cabbage Rolls

- 10 large cabbage leaves
- 1 beaten egg
- ¼ cup tomato juice
- ½ cup chopped onion
- ½ cup soft bread crumbs
- ½ cup quick-cooking rice
- ½ cup chopped fresh mushrooms
- 1 tablespoon paprika
- ½ teaspoon garlic salt
- ½ teaspoon dried thyme, crushed
- ¼ teaspoon pepper
- 1 pound lean ground beef
- ¾ cup tomato juice
- 1 cup dairy sour cream
- 1 tablespoon all-purpose flour

Cut about 2 inches of heavy vein out of each cabbage leaf. Immerse leaves in boiling water for 3 minutes or till limp; drain.

In bowl combine egg, ¼ cup tomato juice, onion, bread crumbs, rice, mushrooms, paprika, garlic salt, thyme, and pepper. Add ground beef; mix well. Place about ¼ *cup* meat mixture in center of each cabbage leaf. Fold in sides and roll ends over meat. Fasten with wooden picks, if desired. Place in large skillet. Add the ¾ cup tomato juice. Bring to boiling. Reduce heat; simmer, covered, 45 minutes. Carefully remove cabbage rolls from skillet onto a warm platter. Skim excess fat from pan juices. Combine sour cream and flour; stir into liquid in skillet. Cook and stir till thickened and heated through. Remove wooden picks from cabbage rolls. Pour sauce over cabbage rolls and serve immediately. Makes 5 servings.

Spaghetti Casserole

7 ounces spaghetti
1 pound ground beef
1 16-ounce can stewed tomatoes
1 15-ounce can tomato sauce
2 teaspoons Italian seasoning
1 teaspoon sugar
1 teaspoon salt
¼ teaspoon garlic powder
¼ teaspoon pepper
1 4-ounce can sliced mushrooms, drained
½ cup sliced pitted ripe olives
¼ cup sliced green onion
2 tablespoons cooking oil
1 cup shredded mozzarella cheese
   (4 ounces)
2 tablespoons snipped parsley

Cook spaghetti according to package directions; drain and set aside. Meanwhile, in a 10-inch skillet cook ground beef till browned; drain off excess fat. Stir in *undrained* tomatoes, tomato sauce, Italian seasoning, sugar, salt, garlic powder, and pepper. Bring to boiling. Reduce heat; simmer, uncovered, 10 minutes.

To cooked spaghetti add mushrooms, olives, green onion, and cooking oil; toss to mix. Layer *half* of the spaghetti mixture into a 12x7½x2-inch baking dish; top with *half* the meat mixture. Repeat layers. Bake, covered, in 350° oven for 20 minutes. Sprinkle with mozzarella cheese; bake, uncovered, 5 to 10 minutes more or till heated through. Sprinkle with parsley. Makes 6 servings.

To stir-fry, use a long-handled spoon or spatula to frequently lift and turn the food with a folding motion.

Stir-Fry Meatball Skillet

1 8¼-ounce can pineapple slices
1 tablespoon soy sauce
2 tablespoons cornstarch
1 beaten egg
2 tablespoons water
2 tablespoons soy sauce
1½ cups soft bread crumbs
1 teaspoon minced dried onion
1 pound ground beef
2 tablespoons cooking oil
2 cups bias-sliced celery
6 green onions, bias sliced into 1-inch
   lengths
1 green pepper, cut into ¾-inch chunks
1 clove garlic, minced
1 10½-ounce can condensed beef broth
2 tablespoons dry sherry
1 tomato, cut into thin wedges
Chow mein noodles (optional)

Drain pineapple, reserving ⅓ cup syrup. Cut two of the pineapple slices into 24 pieces (12 pieces each); set aside. Reserve remaining slices for garnish, if desired, or for another use. In a small mixing bowl blend the reserved pineapple syrup and the 1 tablespoon soy sauce into the cornstarch; set aside. In a mixing bowl combine beaten egg, water, the 2 tablespoons soy sauce, the bread crumbs, and minced dried onion. Add ground beef; mix well. With moistened hands, mold about 1 rounded tablespoon of the meat mixture around each piece of pineapple to make 24 meatballs. In a 12-inch skillet slowly brown meatballs in hot oil 8 to 10 minutes or till nearly done. Remove meatballs and set aside. Drain off all but 2 tablespoons of the drippings.

To the hot drippings in skillet add the celery, onions, green pepper, and garlic. Stir-fry over high heat for 3 to 4 minutes or till vegetables are crisp-tender. Stir soy mixture. Add soy mixture, broth, and sherry to skillet; cook and stir till thickened and bubbly. Return meatballs to skillet; reduce heat. Cover; cook 5 minutes more. Add tomato; cover and cook 1 to 2 minutes or till heated through. If desired, serve over chow mein noodles and garnish with pineapple slices. Makes 4 servings.

Bulgur-Ground Beef Casserole

    1 pound ground beef
    2 stalks celery, chopped (1 cup)
    1 large green pepper, chopped
    1 medium onion, chopped
    1 clove garlic, minced
    1 16-ounce can tomatoes, cut up
    1 cup bulgur wheat
    ½ cup raisins
    ⅓ cup shelled sunflower seed

In a 10-inch skillet cook beef, celery, green pepper, onion, garlic, 1½ teaspoons *salt,* and ⅛ teaspoon *pepper* till meat is browned; drain off excess fat. Stir in *undrained* tomatoes, *uncooked* bulgur, raisins, sunflower seed, and 1 cup *water.* Turn mixture into a 2-quart casserole. Bake, covered, in 375° oven about 35 minutes or till bulgur is tender. Serves 6.

Double-Decker Dinner

    3 eggs
    ½ cup tomato juice
    1½ cups soft bread crumbs
    1 pound ground beef
    1 10-ounce package frozen chopped
        broccoli
    1 cup quick-cooking rice
    1½ teaspoons minced dried onion
    1 cup milk
    1 cup shredded American cheese
        (4 ounces)

In mixing bowl beat *1* of the eggs; stir in the tomato juice, bread crumbs, ¾ teaspoon *salt,* and dash *pepper.* Add meat; mix well. Pat meat evenly in the bottom of an ungreased 8x8x2-inch baking pan or dish. Bake in 350° oven for 20 minutes; spoon off any excess juices.

Meanwhile, in a 1½-quart saucepan cook broccoli in *1¼ cups* boiling *water* according to package directions. *Do not drain.* Stir in rice, onion, and 1 teaspoon *salt;* bring to boiling. Remove from heat. Cover and let stand 5 minutes. Beat the 2 remaining eggs. Stir in beaten eggs, milk, and *half* the cheese. Spread over baked meat. Return to 350° oven; bake 30 minutes more or till rice mixture is firm. Sprinkle remaining cheese atop. Let stand 10 minutes before serving. Makes 6 servings.

Zucchini-Beef Bake

    4 cups thinly sliced zucchini
    2 tablespoons water
    1 4-ounce can sliced mushrooms, drained
    ¾ pound ground beef
    ¼ cup chopped onion
    ¼ cup chopped green pepper
    1 clove garlic, minced
    1 cup cooked barley
    1 8-ounce can tomato sauce
    ½ teaspoon dried oregano, crushed
    1 beaten egg
    1 cup dry cottage cheese *or* cream-style
        cottage cheese, drained
    1 cup soft bread crumbs
    2 tablespoons grated Parmesan cheese
    2 tablespoons butter *or* margarine, melted

In covered large skillet cook zucchini in the water over medium heat for 1 to 2 minutes or till tender; drain well. Remove from skillet; combine with mushrooms and set aside. In same skillet cook ground beef, onion, green pepper, and garlic till beef is brown and vegetables are tender. Drain off excess fat. Stir in cooked barley, tomato sauce, oregano, ½ teaspoon *salt,* and ¼ teaspoon *pepper.* Combine egg and cottage cheese. Arrange *half* of the zucchini-mushroom mixture in the bottom of an 8x8x2-inch baking dish. Spoon meat mixture over. Spread the cottage cheese mixture over the meat mixture. Top with the remaining zucchini-mushroom mixture. Combine bread crumbs, Parmesan, and melted butter or margarine; sprinkle atop casserole. Bake in 350° oven for 30 to 35 minutes or till heated through. Serves 4 or 5.

Containers for Casseroles

Using the correct baking container is important in making a good casserole. For best results, use the dish the recipe recommends. If you do substitute, remember that food may bubble over if baked in too small a dish; if the container is too large, food can dry out. Also keep in mind that food prepared in a deep casserole requires more cooking time than that cooked in a shallow one.

Taco Casserole

1 pound ground beef
½ cup chopped onion
1 8-ounce can tomato sauce
⅓ cup water
1 1¼-ounce envelope taco seasoning mix
2 eggs
1 cup milk
1 16-ounce can red kidney beans, drained
1½ cups shredded Monterey Jack cheese
10 taco *or* tostada shells, coarsely crushed (2½ cups)
1 cup shredded lettuce
½ cup shredded Monterey Jack cheese
1 small tomato, chopped
¼ cup sliced pitted ripe olives

In large skillet cook ground beef and the onion till beef is browned. Drain off excess fat. Stir tomato sauce, water, and taco seasoning mix into meat mixture; heat through. Remove from heat.

Beat eggs; stir in milk. Add a small amount of the tomato sauce mixture to the egg mixture, stirring constantly. Return all to skillet. Stir in kidney beans, the 1½ cups Monterey Jack, and the crushed taco or tostada shells. Turn into a 12x7½x2-inch baking dish.

Bake in a 350° oven about 30 minutes. Top with lettuce, ½ cup cheese, tomato, and olives. Let stand 5 to 10 minutes before cutting into squares. Makes 6 servings.

Savory Beef Pie

Pastry Topping
 1 **cup sliced carrot**
 1 **cup chopped potato**
 1 **4-ounce can mushroom stems and**
   pieces, drained
 ½ **cup chopped onion**
 ¼ **cup chopped green pepper**
 1 **clove garlic, minced**
 3 **tablespoons butter *or* margarine**
 ¼ **cup all-purpose flour**
 ½ **teaspoon salt**
 ¼ **teaspoon pepper**
 ¼ **teaspoon dried thyme, crushed**
 ¼ **teaspoon ground nutmeg**
1½ **cups beef broth**
 2 **cups cubed cooked roast beef**
 1 **cup frozen peas**

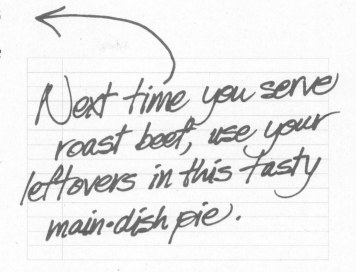

Next time you serve roast beef, use your leftovers in this tasty main-dish pie.

Prepare the dough for the Pastry Topping and set aside.

In 2-quart covered saucepan cook sliced carrot, chopped potato, mushrooms, chopped onion, chopped green pepper, and minced garlic in butter or margarine over medium heat for 5 minutes, stirring occasionally. Stir in flour, salt, pepper, thyme, and nutmeg. Stir in beef broth. Cook, stirring constantly, till thickened and bubbly. Cook and stir 1 to 2 minutes more. Stir in cubed cooked beef and frozen peas. Remove from heat; set aside.

On lightly floured surface roll Pastry Topping to about ⅛-inch thickness. Turn hot beef mixture into 1½-quart casserole; top with pastry. Trim pastry to ½ inch beyond rim; turn under and flute. Cut slits in pastry for escape of steam. Bake in 425° oven for 30 to 35 minutes or till pastry is golden. Makes 4 servings.

Pastry Topping: In a mixing bowl stir together 1¼ cups all-purpose *flour* and ½ teaspoon *salt*. Cut in ⅓ cup *shortening or lard* till pieces are the size of small peas. Sprinkle 1 tablespoon *cold water* over part of the mixture; gently toss with a fork. Push to side of bowl. Repeat with an additional 2 to 3 tablespoons *cold water* till all is moistened. Form dough into a ball.

Swiss Steak and Rice Bake

1½ **pounds beef round steak, cut ¾ inch**
   thick
 ¼ **cup all-purpose flour**
 1 **teaspoon salt**
 ½ **teaspoon dried marjoram, crushed**
 ½ **teaspoon dried thyme, crushed**
 2 **tablespoons shortening**
 1 **28-ounce can tomatoes, cut up**
 1 **cup quick-cooking rice**
 ½ **cup finely chopped celery**
 ½ **cup finely chopped carrot**
 ⅓ **cup water**
 ½ **teaspoon Worcestershire sauce**

Cut meat into 6 serving-size pieces. Combine flour, salt, marjoram, and thyme. Divide *1 tablespoon* flour mixture between the 6 pieces of meat and sprinkle atop; pound each piece with a meat mallet. Turn each piece of meat over and repeat, using *1 tablespoon* flour mixture. In large skillet brown meat on both sides in hot shortening. Transfer meat to a 12x7½x2-inch baking dish. Stir remaining flour mixture into pan drippings. Stir in *undrained* tomatoes, rice, celery, carrot, water, and Worcestershire. Cook and stir till thickened and bubbly; pour over meat.

Bake, covered, in 350° oven about 1 hour and 20 minutes or till meat and rice are tender. Makes 6 servings.

Sausage-Spinach Skillet Pancake

4 **eggs**
1 **cup milk**
1 **cup all-purpose flour**
½ **pound bulk Italian sausage**
½ **cup chopped onion**
2 **cloves garlic, minced**
½ **teaspoon dried basil, crushed**
½ **teaspoon dried thyme, crushed**
3 **cups torn spinach**
2 **tablespoons cooking oil**
⅓ **cup grated Parmesan cheese**

For pancake mixture, place eggs in blender container. Cover; blend at high speed for 1 minute. Reduce speed to medium; with lid ajar, gradually add milk, then the flour and ½ teaspoon *salt.* Blend 30 seconds more. Set aside.

In an oven-proof 10-inch skillet cook sausage, onion, and garlic till sausage is browned. Drain off excess fat. Stir in basil, thyme, and ¼ teaspoon *pepper;* mix well. Add spinach; cover and cook till spinach wilts. Uncover; cook and stir 3 minutes more. Remove from heat. Stir in cooking oil. Immediately pour reserved pancake mixture over sausage mixture. Sprinkle with Parmesan cheese. Bake in a 425° oven for 20 minutes or till puffy and lightly browned. Serve immediately. Makes 4 servings.

Tips for Cooking Pasta

Use plenty of water for cooking pasta. A small amount of cooking oil (1 teaspoon per quart of water) can be added to help prevent sticking.

When water boils vigorously, add pasta a little at a time so the water continues to boil, stir a moment to separate the pieces.

Hold long pasta, such as spaghetti, at one end and dip the other end into the water. As pasta softens, gently curl it around in pan till immersed.

Cook pasta till tender but still slightly firm. Taste near end of cooking to test for doneness. Drain at once.

Spinach Spaghetti Pie

pictured on cover

6 **ounces spaghetti**
2 **tablespoons butter** *or* **margarine**
2 **beaten eggs**
⅓ **cup grated Parmesan cheese**

1 **pound bulk pork sausage**
½ **cup chopped onion**
1 **8-ounce can tomato sauce**
1 **cup cream-style cottage cheese**
1 **3-ounce package cream cheese, softened**
2 **beaten eggs**
¼ **cup grated Parmesan cheese**
1 **10-ounce package frozen chopped spinach, thawed and drained**

¼ **cup soft bread cubes (about ½ slice)**
1 **tablespoon butter** *or* **margarine, melted**

In saucepan cook spaghetti in a large amount of boiling salted water for 10 to 12 minutes or just till tender; drain (should have about 3 cups cooked spaghetti). Stir the 2 tablespoons butter or margarine into the hot cooked spaghetti. Stir in 2 beaten eggs and the ⅓ cup grated Parmesan cheese. Form spaghetti mixture into a "crust" in a greased 10-inch pie plate.

In a skillet cook pork sausage and chopped onion till meat is browned and onion is tender; drain off excess fat. Stir in the tomato sauce. Spread meat mixture over the spaghetti crust.

Combine the cottage cheese and cream cheese. Stir in the 2 eggs and *half* of the remaining Parmesan cheese; set remaining Parmesan cheese aside. Fold spinach into cheese mixture; spoon atop meat mixture. Bake in a 350° oven for 20 minutes.

Combine bread cubes, the 1 tablespoon butter or margarine, and the remaining Parmesan cheese. Sprinkle atop cheese-spinach mixture. Return to oven and bake 8 to 10 minutes more or till bread cubes brown and filling is set. Let stand 5 to 10 minutes before cutting. Makes 6 servings.

Polish Sausage-Kraut Skillet

- 1 medium onion, sliced
- 2 cloves garlic, minced
- 2 tablespoons butter *or* margarine
- 2 medium potatoes, peeled and sliced
- 1 cup sliced carrots
- 1 cup water
- 2 teaspoons instant beef bouillon granules
- 1 teaspoon sugar
- 1 teaspoon caraway seed
- 1 16-ounce can sauerkraut, rinsed and drained
- 5 precooked Polish sausages (about 1 pound)
- 2 teaspoons all-purpose flour
- 1 cup dairy sour cream
  Parsley

In a 12-inch skillet cook onion and garlic in butter or margarine till onion is tender but not brown. Stir in potatoes, carrots, water, bouillon granules, sugar, and caraway seed. Bring to boiling; reduce heat. Cover and simmer 10 to 15 minutes or till vegetables are tender. Place sauerkraut and Polish sausages atop vegetables. Cover; cook 15 minutes more or till sausages are heated through. Stir flour into sour cream; stir into the sausage-kraut mixture and heat through. Season to taste with salt and pepper. Garnish with parsley. Makes 5 servings.

Asparagus-Mushroom Pork Pie

1 slightly beaten egg
¼ cup chili sauce
2 tablespoons water
1 cup bite-size shredded bran squares, slightly crushed (¾ cup crushed)
2 tablespoons finely chopped onion
1 teaspoon salt
1½ pounds lean ground pork

1 pound fresh asparagus, cut up or one 10-ounce package frozen cut asparagus
1 cup sliced fresh mushrooms
2 tablespoons butter or margarine
2 tablespoons all-purpose flour
1 teaspoon instant chicken bouillon granules
¾ cup water
¼ cup dry white wine

In a bowl combine the egg, chili sauce, and the 2 tablespoons water. Mix in the bran cereal, onion, and salt; let stand 5 minutes or till cereal absorbs the liquid. Add ground pork; mix well. Using the back of a spoon, press meat mixture over bottom and sides of an inverted 9-inch pie plate to form a shell. Cover with foil. Bake in a 375° oven for 20 minutes. (Place a shallow baking pan on lower oven rack directly under pie plate to catch drippings.) Uncover and bake 15 minutes more or till meat is done. Let stand 5 minutes.

Meanwhile, cook fresh asparagus in a small amount of boiling, salted water for 8 to 10 minutes; drain. (Or, cook frozen asparagus in a small amount of boiling, salted water according to package directions; drain.)

In a saucepan cook mushrooms in butter or margarine for 3 to 4 minutes or till tender. Stir in flour and bouillon granules. Stir in the ¾ cup water and the wine; cook and stir till mixture is thickened and bubbly. Remove fat from meat shell with turkey baster. Place meat shell upright on serving platter. Arrange asparagus in meat shell. Pour some of the mushroom sauce over all; pass remaining sauce. Cut pie into wedges to serve. Makes 6 servings.

Chorizo-Stuffed Eggplant

3 medium eggplants (1 pound each)
1¼ pounds bulk chorizo or bulk Italian sausage, crumbled
1 small onion, thinly sliced
1 medium green pepper, cut into strips
1 tablespoon snipped chives
¾ teaspoon dried oregano, crushed
⅓ cup grated Parmesan cheese
2 medium tomatoes, sliced and halved Cooking oil

Halve eggplants lengthwise. Carefully scoop out pulp, leaving a ½-inch-thick shell; reserve pulp. Cook eggplant shells, uncovered, in a large pan of boiling water 2 minutes or till tender. Drain; sprinkle with salt. Set aside. In large skillet cook sausage over low heat 5 minutes; drain. Stir next 4 ingredients and ¼ teaspoon *pepper* into skillet; cook till vegetables are tender. Chop reserved eggplant pulp; add to sausage mixture. Cook, covered, 5 minutes; spoon into eggplant shells. Sprinkle cheese atop. Place shells in an ungreased 15x10x1-inch shallow baking pan; cover lightly with foil. Bake in a 350° oven for 20 minutes; remove foil. Place tomato slice halves atop; brush lightly with oil. Bake, uncovered, 5 to 10 minutes more. Serves 6.

Pork and Bean Casserole

1½ pounds pork cubed steaks
½ cup chopped onion
1 clove garlic, minced
2 tablespoons cooking oil
2 21-ounce cans pork and beans in tomato sauce
1 teaspoon chili powder
¼ teaspoon dried oregano, crushed
1 medium tomato, sliced and halved
½ cup shredded American cheese

Cut steaks into bite-size pieces. Quickly brown meat, onion, and garlic in hot oil. Add beans, chili powder, and oregano. Turn into a 2-quart casserole. Bake in a 350° oven for 45 minutes. Remove from oven; stir. Place tomato slice halves atop casserole. Bake 15 minutes more. Top with cheese; bake 2 to 3 minutes or till cheese melts. Serve in soup plates. Makes 6 servings.

Spicy Pork 'n' Sausage Dinner

6 pork chops, cut 1 inch thick
¼ cup all-purpose flour
2 teaspoons caraway seed
3 tablespoons cooking oil
3 medium potatoes, peeled and cut
    into chunks
4 ounces knockwurst, diced
1 cup chopped celery
½ cup chopped onion
2 small sweet pickles, finely chopped
1 cup beef broth
⅓ cup tomato paste

Trim fat from chops. Combine flour, caraway, and 1½ teaspoons *salt*. Coat both sides of chops with flour mixture. In 12-inch skillet brown chops in hot oil; drain off excess fat. Add potatoes, knockwurst, celery, onion, and pickles. Stir broth into tomato paste along with ¼ teaspoon *pepper;* pour over vegetables and chops. Simmer, covered, 40 minutes or till meat and vegetables are tender. Skim off excess fat. Makes 6 servings.

Pork Chop and Rice Bake

4 pork chops, cut ½ inch thick
1 tablespoon cooking oil *or* shortening
1 7½-ounce can semi-condensed cream
    of mushroom soup
½ cup dry white wine
⅔ cup long grain rice
1 4-ounce can sliced mushrooms, drained
1 teaspoon instant beef bouillon granules
1 teaspoon Worcestershire sauce
¼ teaspoon garlic powder
¼ teaspoon dried thyme, crushed
1 small onion, thinly sliced and separated
    into rings
   Snipped parsley

In a 12-inch skillet brown chops on both sides in oil. Season with pepper. In an 8x8x2-inch baking dish combine soup, wine, and ½ cup *water;* stir in *uncooked* rice, mushrooms, bouillon granules, Worcestershire, garlic powder, and thyme. Top with pork chops, then add onion rings. Cover and bake in a 375° oven for 60 minutes or till chops are tender. Trim with parsley. Makes 4 servings.

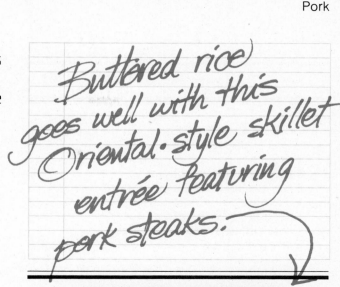

Buttered rice goes well with this Oriental-style skillet entrée featuring pork steaks.

Oriental-Style Pork Steaks

1½ pounds pork steaks, cut ½ inch thick
1 tablespoon cooking oil
1 8-ounce can crushed pineapple
    (juice pack)
2 tablespoons soy sauce
2 tablespoons vinegar
1 teaspoon sugar
½ teaspoon ground ginger
4 medium carrots, bias sliced ¼ inch thick
    (2 cups)
½ small onion, cut into wedges
1 small green pepper, seeded and cut into
    bite-size strips
1½ teaspoons cornstarch

Cut pork steaks into 4 serving-size portions. In 10-inch skillet brown pork steaks on both sides in hot oil. Remove from skillet and set aside. Drain excess fat from skillet.

Drain the crushed pineapple, reserving juice; add enough water to juice to make ½ cup liquid. Combine pineapple juice mixture with soy sauce, vinegar, sugar, and ground ginger. Add to skillet along with the carrots and onion. Return the browned pork steaks to skillet; cover and simmer 20 to 25 minutes or till meat and carrots are tender. Add green pepper strips, stirring into sauce. Cover and simmer about 3 minutes. Remove steaks from skillet; keep warm.

Combine the crushed pineapple and the cornstarch; add to vegetables and juices in skillet. Cook and stir till mixture is thickened and bubbly. Cook and stir 1 to 2 minutes more. Return steaks to skillet; spoon sauce over. Serves 4.

Fiesta Ham Pie

2 cups fully cooked ham cut into strips
½ cup chopped onion
⅓ cup chopped green pepper
2 tablespoons cooking oil
2 tablespoons all-purpose flour
1 8-ounce can whole kernel corn
1 8-ounce can tomato sauce
¼ cup sliced pitted ripe olives
½ of a 1¼-ounce envelope (2 tablespoons)
    taco seasoning mix
1 8-ounce package corn muffin mix
½ cup shredded cheddar cheese

In large saucepan cook ham, onion, and green pepper in hot oil till onion is tender but not brown. Stir in flour. Stir in *undrained* corn, tomato sauce, olives, taco seasoning mix, and 1 cup *water*. Heat to boiling, stirring constantly. Prepare corn muffin mix according to package directions; stir in cheese. Pour tomato mixture into a 9x9x2-inch baking pan. Top with spoonfuls of muffin batter. Bake in a 375° oven for 25 minutes or till golden. Makes 6 servings.

Italian Pork Casserole

1 medium green pepper
2 cups cubed cooked pork
1 15-ounce can tomato sauce
1 14½-ounce can beef broth
1 cup long grain rice
½ cup chopped onion
1 4-ounce can sliced mushrooms, drained
1 teaspoon sugar
1 teaspoon dried basil, crushed
½ teaspoon dried oregano, crushed
¼ teaspoon garlic powder
½ cup shredded mozzarella cheese

Cut 3 slices from the green pepper; chop the remaining pepper. In a 10-inch skillet combine the chopped green pepper, pork, tomato sauce, beef broth, uncooked rice, onion, mushrooms, sugar, basil, oregano, garlic powder, and ⅛ teaspoon *pepper.* Stir thoroughly. Bring to boiling; reduce heat and simmer, covered, 20 minutes or till rice is tender. Stir occasionally. Sprinkle mozzarella cheese around edge of skillet. Trim with green pepper slices. Makes 6 servings.

Pork Crepes

½ cup all-purpose flour
¾ cup milk
1 egg
1½ teaspoons cooking oil
⅛ teaspoon salt

1 pound ground pork
1 15-ounce can tomato sauce
2 teaspoons minced dried onion
½ teaspoon dried marjoram, crushed
½ teaspoon dried thyme, crushed
½ teaspoon salt
1 10-ounce package frozen peas
    and carrots
½ cup shredded mozzarella cheese
    (2 ounces)

For crepes, in a bowl combine flour, milk, egg, oil, and the ⅛ teaspoon salt; beat with rotary beater till well blended. Heat a lightly greased and seasoned 6-inch skillet. Remove from heat; spoon 2 tablespoons of the batter into hot skillet. Lift and tilt skillet to spread batter evenly. Return to heat; brown crepe on one side only. To remove crepe, invert pan over paper toweling; remove crepe. Repeat with remaining batter to make about 8 crepes, greasing skillet as necessary. Set crepes aside while preparing filling.

For filling, in a 10-inch skillet brown ground pork; drain off excess fat. Stir in the tomato sauce, onion, marjoram, thyme, and the ½ teaspoon salt. Bring mixture to boiling; reduce heat. Cover and simmer for 5 minutes. Stir in peas and carrots. Bring to boiling; reduce heat. Cover and cook 8 to 10 minutes or till vegetables are tender.

Spoon about ⅓ *cup* of the meat mixture down the center of *each* crepe. Fold two top edges so they overlap atop filling. Place crepes seam side down in a 12x7½x2-inch baking dish. Top with remaining meat mixture. Bake in a 350° oven for 10 minutes. Sprinkle with mozzarella cheese; continue baking 5 to 10 minutes more or till the cheese is melted and the crepes are heated through. Makes 4 servings.

Crusty buttered rolls and Thousand Island dressing spooned over lettuce wedges will round out this fruited skillet meal.

Fruited Pork Skillet

1 15¼-ounce can pineapple chunks
  (juice pack)
1½ pounds boneless pork, cut into
  ½-inch cubes
2 tablespoons cooking oil
2¼ cups water
¼ cup vinegar
3 tablespoons soy sauce
1 tablespoon brown sugar
2 teaspoons instant chicken
  bouillon granules
¼ teaspoon ground ginger

---

1 cup long grain rice
4 green onions, diagonally cut into
  1-inch pieces
1 medium green pepper, cut into
  1-inch squares
1 11-ounce can mandarin orange
  sections, drained

Drain pineapple chunks, reserving ½ cup of the juice. Set pineapple and juice aside. In a 10-inch skillet cook the pork cubes in hot cooking oil till browned. Drain off excess fat. Stir in water, the reserved ½ cup pineapple juice, the vinegar, soy sauce, brown sugar, chicken bouillon granules, and ginger. Cover and simmer over low heat for 20 minutes. Stir in the uncooked rice and green onions. Cover and continue cooking about 20 minutes or till rice and meat are tender. Add green pepper squares; cover and cook 5 minutes more. Stir in pineapple chunks; sprinkle orange sections on top. Heat through. Makes 6 servings.

Chinese Pork Bake

1 pound boneless pork
½ cup all-purpose flour
½ teaspoon paprika
¼ teaspoon salt
¼ teaspoon pepper
2 tablespoons cooking oil

½ cup chopped onion
¼ cup chopped green pepper
1 16-ounce can fancy mixed Chinese
  vegetables, drained
1 10¾-ounce can condensed cream of
  mushroom soup
1 4-ounce can sliced mushrooms, drained
2 tablespoons soy sauce
¼ teaspoon ground ginger
1 3-ounce package Oriental noodles with
  pork seasoning

¾ cup soft bread crumbs (1 slice)
¼ cup slivered almonds
2 tablespoons butter *or* margarine, melted

Partially freeze pork; thinly slice across the grain into bite-size strips. In medium bowl combine flour, paprika, salt, and pepper. Add pork strips, half at a time, and toss to coat. In large skillet cook *half* the pork in hot oil till browned; remove from skillet. Add additional cooking oil, if necessary. Cook remaining pork strips with onion and green pepper till meat is browned. Return all meat to skillet. Stir in the Chinese vegetables, condensed mushroom soup, mushrooms, soy sauce, and ginger. Set aside.

Cook the noodles in boiling *unsalted* water for 3 minutes or just till tender; drain. Stir cooked noodles into pork mixture along with the seasoning mix from the noodles. Turn mixture into a greased 2-quart casserole.

Combine the bread crumbs, almonds, and melted butter or margarine; sprinkle atop the casserole. Bake in a 350° oven for 45 minutes or till heated through. Makes 4 to 6 servings.

Lamb and Bulgur Skillet

1 pound boneless lamb, cut into
   ¾-inch cubes
2 tablespoons olive oil **or** cooking oil
2 cups chicken broth
½ cup sliced green onion
3 cloves garlic, minced
1 teaspoon salt
1 teaspoon dried oregano, crushed
   Dash pepper
1 cup bulgur wheat
2 medium zucchini, halved lengthwise
   and sliced (3cups)

In a 10-inch skillet brown lamb in hot oil. Add chicken broth, onion, garlic, salt, oregano, and pepper. Bring mixture to boiling. Reduce heat; cover and simmer 15 minutes. Stir in bulgur; cover and simmer 15 minutes more. Stir in zucchini; cover and simmer 10 minutes more or till bulgur and meat are tender. Makes 4 servings.

Eggplant Casserole

1 pound ground lamb
1 cup chopped onion
1½ cups coarsely chopped peeled eggplant
1 cup coarsely chopped potato
½ cup tomato sauce
1 teaspoon chili powder
¾ teaspoon ground nutmeg
½ teaspoon salt
½ teaspoon garlic powder
¼ cup grated Parmesan cheese
2 eggs
1 cup plain yogurt
   Snipped parsley

In a 10-inch skillet cook lamb and onion till meat is browned and onion is tender. Drain off excess fat. Stir in eggplant, potato, tomato sauce, chili powder, nutmeg, salt, and garlic powder. Simmer, covered, for 20 minutes or till eggplant and potato are tender. Stir in the cheese. Spoon mixture into a 1½-quart casserole. Beat together eggs and yogurt. Spoon atop eggplant mixture. Bake in a 350° oven for 30 to 35 minutes or till top is set. Sprinkle with the snipped parsley. Serves 6.

Lamb-Potato Pie

1½ pounds boneless lamb, cut into 1-inch
   cubes
3 tablespoons cooking oil
1 cup water
2 teaspoons instant beef bouillon granules
¾ teaspoon dried thyme, crushed
1 cup sliced fresh mushrooms
¼ cup chopped onion
2 medium carrots, sliced
2 medium zucchini, sliced
½ cup cold water
2 tablespoons all-purpose flour

3 cups hot mashed potatoes
¼ cup butter **or** margarine, cut up
2 eggs
¼ teaspoon salt
   Dash pepper
   Paprika

In a Dutch oven brown lamb cubes, half at a time, in hot cooking oil. Drain off excess fat. Return all meat to Dutch oven. Stir in the 1 cup water, the beef bouillon granules, and thyme; mix well. Add mushrooms and onion. Bring to boiling; reduce heat. Cover and simmer 45 minutes. Add sliced carrots and simmer, covered, 15 minutes more. Stir in the zucchini slices. Combine the ½ cup cold water and the all-purpose flour; stir into the meat mixture. Cook and stir till mixture is thickened and bubbly. Turn lamb-vegetable mixture into a 10-inch pie plate.

In a mixer bowl combine the hot mashed potatoes, butter or margarine, eggs, salt, and pepper. Beat at medium speed of electric mixer till thoroughly combined. Dollop the potato mixture around the edge of meat mixture in pie plate. (Or, use a pastry tube to pipe the potato mixture around the edge of the pie plate.) Sprinkle potatoes with paprika. Bake in a 425° oven for 15 minutes. Makes 6 servings.

Lamb and Vegetable Skillet

4 lamb rib chops, loin chops, *or* leg sirloin chops (1¼ pounds)
1 tablespoon cooking oil
⅛ teaspoon garlic powder
⅛ teaspoon dried marjoram, crushed
⅛ teaspoon pepper
½ cup water
1 teaspoon instant chicken bouillon granules
8 tiny new potatoes *or* 2 medium potatoes, peeled and quartered
2 small zucchini, cut into ½-inch pieces
2 small onions, sliced
1 medium green pepper, cut into strips
¼ teaspoon salt
⅛ teaspoon pepper
2 medium tomatoes, cut into wedges
1 tablespoon snipped parsley

In a 12-inch skillet brown lamb chops in hot cooking oil. Drain off excess fat. Sprinkle meat with garlic powder, marjoram, and pepper. Stir in water and bouillon granules. Bring to boiling; reduce heat. Simmer, covered, 10 minutes.

Arrange potatoes around chops. Simmer, covered, 20 minutes more or till potatoes are almost tender. Add the zucchini, onions, and green pepper. Sprinkle vegetables with the salt and pepper. Simmer, covered, 10 minutes more or till zucchini and green pepper are crisp-tender. Add the tomato wedges and cook, covered, 3 minutes more or till heated through. Sprinkle with snipped parsley. Serve from skillet with pan juices spooned over each serving. Makes 4 servings.

Potted Lamb and Vegetables

1 3-pound boneless lamb shoulder roast
2 tablespoons cooking oil
1 tablespoon snipped parsley
¾ teaspoon dried dillweed
½ teaspoon dried oregano, crushed
1 10½-ounce can condensed beef broth
¾ cup dry red wine
1 pound tiny new potatoes
6 medium carrots, cut into 1-inch pieces
1 medium onion, sliced
2 tablespoons cornstarch

In Dutch oven brown meat on all sides in hot oil. Sprinkle meat with parsley, dillweed, oregano, ½ teaspoon *pepper,* and ¼ teaspoon *salt.* Pour broth and wine over all. Cover; simmer 1½ hours.

Peel a strip around each potato. Add vegetables to meat. Cover; simmer 20 minutes more or till tender. Slice meat; place on platter with vegetables. Cover; keep warm. Skim fat from cooking liquid. Measure 1¾ cups cooking liquid; return to pan. Blend ¼ cup *cold water* into cornstarch; stir into liquid. Cook and stir till thickened and bubbly. Cook and stir 1 to 2 minutes more. Pass with meat and vegetables. Makes 6 servings.

Lamb and Pasta Bake

1 pound ground lamb
½ cup chopped onion
1 15-ounce can tomato sauce
1 teaspoon dried oregano, crushed
2 medium zucchini, sliced
6 ounces elbow macaroni (1¾ cups), cooked and drained
1½ cups small-curd cream-style cottage cheese
2 cups shredded Monterey Jack cheese

In a 10-inch skillet cook lamb and onion till lamb is browned and onion is tender; drain. Stir in tomato sauce and oregano. Bring to boiling; reduce heat. Stir in zucchini. Cover; simmer 8 minutes. Remove from heat. In greased 12x7½x2-inch baking dish layer *half* the macaroni, *half* the meat, all of the cottage cheese, and *half* the shredded cheese. Repeat layers with macaroni, meat, and shredded cheese. Cover; bake in a 375° oven about 35 minutes or till hot through. Serves 6 to 8.

Lamb-Spinach Pie

pictured on page 5

1 13¾-ounce package hot roll mix
1 pound ground lamb
½ cup chopped onion
1 slightly beaten egg
1 teaspoon dillseed
½ teaspoon salt
¼ teaspoon pepper
¼ teaspoon dried rosemary, crushed
¼ teaspoon dried basil, crushed
¼ teaspoon dried oregano, crushed
¼ cup fine dry bread crumbs

1 slightly beaten egg
1 10-ounce package frozen chopped spinach, thawed and well drained
2⅔ cups crumbled feta cheese (14 ounces)
1½ cups ricotta cheese
¼ teaspoon salt

Prepare hot roll mix according to package directions and let rise. Meanwhile, in skillet cook lamb and onion till meat is browned and onion is tender; drain off excess fat. In bowl combine 1 egg, dillseed, the ½ teaspoon salt, pepper, rosemary, basil, and oregano. Stir in meat and fine dry bread crumbs; set aside.

On lightly floured surface roll ¾ of the dough to a 13-inch circle. Fit in bottom and up sides of a greased 9-inch springform pan. Spoon the meat mixture over the dough.

Reserve *1 tablespoon* of the 1 slightly beaten egg. Pat spinach dry with paper toweling. In medium bowl combine the spinach, remaining slightly beaten egg, feta cheese, ricotta cheese, and the ¼ teaspoon salt. Spread over meat mixture. Roll out the remaining portion of dough to a 9-inch circle; place atop filling. Fold excess bottom dough over top; pinch to seal. Brush with the 1 tablespoon reserved egg. Bake in a 350° oven for 45 to 50 minutes. Cool 10 minutes before serving. Remove sides of springform pan. Makes 6 servings.

Dilled Lamb and Vegetables

1½ pounds boneless lamb, cut into
　　　1-inch cubes
¼ cup all-purpose flour
1 small onion, sliced and separated
　　　into rings
2 tablespoons cooking oil
1 16-ounce can stewed tomatoes
6 medium potatoes, peeled and cut
　　　into 1-inch cubes
3 medium carrots, sliced
½ cup chicken broth
½ cup dry white wine
½ teaspoon dried dillweed

Coat lamb with a mixture of flour, ½ teaspoon *salt,* and ⅛ teaspoon *pepper.* In a 12-inch skillet brown lamb and onion, half at a time, in hot oil. Turn into a 3-quart casserole. Stir in remaining ingredients. Cover; bake in 350° oven for 1½ to 1¾ hours or till tender. Makes 6 servings.

Orange Lamb and Rice Skillet

1½ pounds boneless lamb, cut into
　　　1-inch pieces
1 clove garlic, minced
3 tablespoons cooking oil
½ cup sliced onion
¾ cup brown rice
1 cup orange juice
2 teaspoons instant chicken bouillon
　　　granules
½ teaspoon ground cinnamon
1 medium green pepper, cut into strips
1 11-ounce can mandarin orange sections,
　　　drained
2 tablespoons snipped parsley

In a 10-inch skillet brown lamb and garlic in hot oil. Remove lamb; set aside. Add onion to skillet; cook till tender. Stir in uncooked rice. Continue cooking 4 to 5 minutes; stir frequently. Return lamb to skillet. Stir in orange juice, bouillon granules, cinnamon, and 1 cup *water.* Bring to boiling; reduce heat. Cover; simmer 30 minutes. Add green pepper. Simmer, covered, 30 minutes more or till lamb and rice are tender and liquid is absorbed. Stir in oranges; heat through. Sprinkle with parsley. Makes 6 servings.

Zucchini Lamb Pie

1½ cups shredded zucchini
1 pound ground lamb
½ cup chopped onion
1 clove garlic, minced
2 tablespoons all-purpose flour
1 10-ounce package frozen chopped
　　　spinach, thawed and well drained
¼ cup grated Romano *or* Parmesan cheese
½ teaspoon salt
½ teaspoon dried basil, crushed
¼ teaspoon pepper
1½ cups cream-style cottage cheese,
　　　drained

¼ cup butter *or* margarine
¼ cup all-purpose flour
2 cups milk
3 beaten eggs

In saucepan cook zucchini, covered, in boiling salted water for 1 to 2 minutes. Drain well, pressing out the excess water.

In skillet cook ground lamb, chopped onion, and garlic till lamb is browned and onion is tender; drain off excess fat. Stir in the 2 tablespoons flour; then stir in the well-drained spinach and zucchini, the Romano or Parmesan cheese, salt, basil, and pepper. Spread mixture in the bottom of a 12x7½x2-inch baking dish. Spread cottage cheese over the meat mixture.

In saucepan melt the butter or margarine. Stir in the ¼ cup flour. Add milk all at once. Cook and stir till thickened and bubbly. Cook and stir 1 to 2 minutes more. Slowly stir about *1 cup* of the hot mixture into the beaten eggs; return to remaining hot mixture in the saucepan. Heat mixture through but do not boil.

Remove saucepan from heat. Pour over the cottage cheese layer in baking dish. Bake in a 350° oven for 45 to 50 minutes or till top is set and mixture is heated through. Let stand 5 minutes before serving. Makes 6 servings.

Herbed Chicken and Dumplings

1 2½- to 3-pound broiler-fryer chicken,
    cut up
2 tablespoons cooking oil

---

4 medium carrots, cut into ½-inch pieces
2 cups sliced fresh mushrooms
1 cup frozen small whole onions, thawed
¾ cup dry white wine
¾ cup water
¼ cup snipped parsley
1 teaspoon salt
1 teaspoon instant chicken bouillon
    granules
½ teaspoon dried marjoram, crushed
½ teaspoon dried thyme, crushed
¼ teaspoon garlic powder
1 bay leaf

---

1 cup packaged biscuit mix
2 tablespoons snipped parsley
⅓ cup milk

---

1 cup dairy sour cream
2 tablespoons all-purpose flour

In Dutch oven cook chicken pieces in hot oil till well browned. Drain off excess fat. Add carrots, sliced mushrooms, thawed onions, wine, water, ¼ cup parsley, salt, bouillon granules, marjoram, thyme, garlic powder, and bay leaf. Bring to boiling; reduce heat. Cover and simmer 50 minutes or till chicken is tender. Remove bay leaf and spoon off any fat.

For dumplings, in bowl combine biscuit mix and 2 tablespoons parsley. Add the ⅓ cup milk and stir with fork just till moistened.

In small bowl combine the sour cream and flour. Stir into chicken mixture in Dutch oven, mixing well. When chicken mixture is bubbling, drop dumpling mixture from spoon onto hot liquid around edge of pan to make 6 dumplings. Simmer, covered, for 15 minutes. Makes 6 servings.

Use either fresh or dried basil when preparing this Italian-style poultry main dish.

Chicken and Vegetable Skillet

¼ cup all-purpose flour
1 teaspoon salt
¼ teaspoon pepper
1 2½- to 3-pound broiler-fryer chicken,
    cut up
1 small onion, thinly sliced
2 tablespoons cooking oil
⅔ cup chicken broth
⅔ cup dry white wine

1½ cups peeled, cubed eggplant
2 medium tomatoes, peeled and quartered
1 medium green pepper, cut into thin
    strips
1 medium carrot, thinly sliced
3 tablespoons snipped parsley
1 tablespoon snipped fresh basil *or*
    1 teaspoon dried basil, crushed
½ teaspoon salt
¼ teaspoon pepper

In paper or plastic bag combine flour, the 1 teaspoon salt, and ¼ teaspoon pepper. Add chicken, a few pieces at a time; shake to coat. Brown chicken and onion in hot oil about 15 minutes. Spoon off fat. Add chicken broth and wine. Reduce heat; cover and simmer about 10 minutes.

Add eggplant, tomatoes, green pepper, carrot, parsley, basil, the ½ teaspoon salt, and ¼ teaspoon pepper. Cover and cook for 15 to 20 minutes or till chicken and vegetables are tender. Remove chicken and vegetables to serving platter; keep warm. Skim fat off pan juices. Measure pan juices and return to skillet. Boil, uncovered, over high heat till reduced to ¾ cup; pour over chicken and vegetables. Makes 6 servings.

Chicken with Marinated Vegetables

1 10-ounce package frozen whole kernel
  corn, cooked and drained
2 medium tomatoes, coarsely chopped
1½ cups sliced fresh mushrooms
⅓ cup dry white wine
⅓ cup cooking oil
¼ cup sliced green onion
¼ cup snipped parsley
1 tablespoon lemon juice
1 teaspoon dried marjoram, crushed
1 teaspoon dried dillweed
½ teaspoon salt

1¼ cups cornflake crumbs
¼ cup sliced almonds
½ teaspoon paprika
¼ teaspoon salt
¼ teaspoon pepper
1 2½- to 3-pound broiler-fryer chicken,
  cut up
6 tablespoons butter or margarine, melted

In a large bowl combine the corn, chopped tomatoes, sliced mushrooms, wine, cooking oil, sliced green onion, parsley, lemon juice, marjoram, dillweed, and the ½ teaspoon salt. Stir to mix thoroughly. Set vegetable mixture aside to marinate while baking the chicken. Stir the vegetable mixture occasionally.

For crumb mixture, in shallow dish combine the cornflake crumbs, sliced almonds, paprika, the ¼ teaspoon salt, and the pepper; mix well. Brush chicken pieces with melted butter or margarine; then roll in the cornflake crumb mixture, coating evenly. Place crumb-coated chicken pieces, skin side up, in a 13x9x2-inch baking dish.

Bake in a 375° oven for 45 minutes or till chicken is golden and tender. Remove chicken pieces from baking dish; drain off fat. Spoon the *drained* marinated vegetable mixture into the baking dish. Top with chicken pieces. Return to oven and bake 15 minutes more or till vegetables are heated through. Makes 6 servings.

Chicken and Vegetables Paprika

1 2½- to 3-pound broiler-fryer chicken,
  cut up
1 clove garlic, minced
2 tablespoons cooking oil
2 teaspoons paprika
2 teaspoons instant chicken bouillon
  granules
1¼ cups apple juice
4 medium potatoes, peeled and quartered
2 medium parsnips, sliced
2 medium carrots, sliced
½ cup sliced onion
1 medium green pepper, chopped
1 cup dairy sour cream
2 tablespoons all-purpose flour
2 tablespoons snipped parsley

In a 12-inch skillet cook chicken and garlic in hot oil till chicken is browned. Drain off fat. Combine paprika, bouillon granules, ½ teaspoon *salt,* and ⅛ teaspoon *pepper;* sprinkle over chicken. Pour apple juice over all. Bring to boiling; reduce heat. Cover; simmer 15 minutes. Add next 5 ingredients. Cover; simmer 30 minutes or till vegetables are done. Combine sour cream and flour. Push chicken and vegetables to one side of skillet. Stir sour cream mixture into liquid in skillet; blend well. Cook and stir till thickened and bubbly. Sprinkle with parsley. Makes 6 servings.

Seasoning a Skillet

Some skillets need to be seasoned or conditioned before the first use; others require no treatment. Those needing seasoning are iron and some aluminum or alloy skillets.

To season cast iron and other porous metal skillets, lightly rub inside of a clean, dry pan with cooking oil. Heat pan in 250° or 300° oven several hours.

To retain this seasoning from one use to the next, wash skillet well after each use, but do not scour. When scouring is necessary, or after washing in an automatic dishwasher, recondition the skillet.

31

Chicken-Cranberry Pinwheel Bake

2 cups packaged biscuit mix
½ cup milk
½ cup cranberry-orange relish
¼ cup chopped onion
¼ cup butter *or* margarine
⅓ cup all-purpose flour
1 14½-ounce can chicken broth
1⅓ cups milk
1½ cups cooked chicken *or* turkey cut into bite-size pieces
1 cup shredded cheddar cheese (4 ounces)
1 3-ounce can sliced mushrooms, drained

To prepare pinwheels, combine biscuit mix and the ½ cup milk. Stir till well blended. Turn out onto lightly floured surface; knead 5 to 6 times. Roll out to a 10-inch square. Spread cranberry relish over dough to within ½ inch on all sides. Roll up as for jelly roll. Moisten edges with water; seal. Cut into 8 slices; set aside.

In saucepan cook onion in butter or margarine till tender but not brown. Stir in flour, blending well. Add chicken broth and the 1⅓ cups milk. Cook and stir till mixture is thickened and bubbly. Cook and stir 1 to 2 minutes more. Stir in chicken or turkey, cheese, and mushrooms. Cook and stir over low heat till cheese melts and mixture is boiling. Turn chicken mixture into a 12x7½x2-inch baking dish. Arrange pinwheels, cut side down, atop hot mixture. Bake in a 425° oven about 25 minutes or till biscuits are browned. Serves 4 to 6.

Italian Chicken Skillet

½ cup sliced celery
¼ cup chopped green pepper
¼ cup chopped onion
1 clove garlic, minced
2 tablespoons cooking oil
1 16-ounce can stewed tomatoes
1½ cups chopped cooked chicken
1 9-ounce package frozen Italian green beans
⅔ cup quick-cooking rice
1 2½-ounce jar sliced mushrooms
1½ teaspoons Italian seasoning
½ cup shredded mozzarella cheese

In a 10-inch skillet cook celery, green pepper, onion, and garlic in hot oil till tender. Stir in *undrained* tomatoes, chicken, beans, uncooked rice, *undrained* mushrooms, Italian seasoning, ½ teaspoon *salt,* and ⅛ teaspoon *pepper.* Bring to boiling; reduce heat. Cover and simmer 10 minutes or till beans and rice are done. Sprinkle cheese atop. Cover; cook 2 minutes more or till cheese is melted. Serve immediately. Makes 4 servings.

Easy Chicken-Rice Divan

2 10-ounce packages frozen broccoli spears
½ cup grated Parmesan cheese
2 cups cubed cooked chicken *or* turkey
1 cup cooked rice
2 tablespoons butter *or* margarine
2 tablespoons all-purpose flour
1 cup milk
1 tablespoon lemon juice
1 cup dairy sour cream

Cook broccoli according to package directions; drain. Arrange broccoli in 12x7½x2-inch baking dish. Sprinkle with *half* the Parmesan; top with chicken or turkey. Season poultry with salt and pepper; spoon cooked rice over. Melt butter or margarine; blend in flour. Add milk all at once. Cook and stir till bubbly. Cook and stir 2 minutes more. Remove from heat. Stir in lemon juice. Fold in sour cream. Pour sauce evenly over poultry; sprinkle with remaining Parmesan. Bake in a 400° oven for 15 to 18 minutes. Makes 6 servings.

Corn Bread Chicken Casserole

33

1 cup sliced fresh mushrooms
½ cup sliced celery
¼ cup chopped onion
3 tablespoons butter *or* margarine
3 tablespoons all-purpose flour
1⅔ cups milk
1½ teaspoons Worcestershire sauce
1 teaspoon instant chicken bouillon granules
1½ cups cubed cooked chicken

1 beaten egg
½ of a 10-ounce package frozen chopped spinach, thawed and well drained
¾ cup dairy sour cream
¼ cup butter *or* margarine, melted
½ cup all-purpose flour
½ cup yellow cornmeal
1 teaspoon baking powder
¼ teaspoon salt
¾ cup shredded American cheese (3 ounces)

In a large saucepan cook mushrooms, celery, and onion in 3 tablespoons butter or margarine till vegetables are tender but not brown; stir in the 3 tablespoons flour, mixing well. Stir in milk, Worcestershire, and chicken bouillon granules. Cook and stir till thickened and bubbly; cook and stir 1 minute more. Stir in chicken. Keep hot while preparing corn bread.

For corn bread, in a bowl combine egg, spinach, sour cream, and ¼ cup butter or margarine. In another bowl combine flour, cornmeal, baking powder, and salt. Stir into egg mixture till moistened. Turn hot chicken mixture into a 10x6x2-inch baking dish and immediately spread corn bread mixture atop. Bake in a 350° oven for 35 to 40 minutes or till wooden pick inserted in center comes out clean. Sprinkle top with shredded American cheese; bake 2 minutes more or till cheese is melted. Makes 4 servings.

Turkey Eggplant Lasagna

1 beaten egg
¼ cup milk
1 medium eggplant
¾ cup fine dry bread crumbs
6 tablespoons cooking oil

¼ cup chopped onion
1 clove garlic, minced
   Cooking oil
1 15-ounce can tomato sauce
1 7½-ounce can tomatoes, cut up
1 tablespoon dried parsley flakes
1 teaspoon sugar
1 teaspoon dried oregano, crushed
½ teaspoon salt
1½ cups chopped cooked turkey
1½ cups shredded mozzarella cheese
      (6 ounces)
¼ cup grated Parmesan cheese

Combine the egg and milk. Peel and slice the eggplant crosswise into ¼-inch-thick slices. Dip the eggplant slices into the egg mixture, then into the fine dry bread crumbs to coat each eggplant slice.

In a skillet cook eggplant slices, one-third at a time, each time in *2 tablespoons* of the cooking oil, till golden, turning once. Remove the eggplant from the skillet; drain eggplant.

Cook onion and garlic in the skillet till onion is tender but not brown, adding more cooking oil if needed. Stir in the tomato sauce, *undrained* tomatoes, parsley flakes, sugar, oregano, and salt. Bring mixture to boiling; reduce heat. Simmer, covered, 10 minutes. Add the turkey to the sauce. Arrange *half* of the eggplant slices in a 12x7½x2-inch baking dish. Spoon *half* of the tomato-turkey sauce over. Sprinkle with *half* of the mozzarella cheese. Repeat layers of eggplant, sauce, and mozzarella. Sprinkle Parmesan cheese atop. Bake, covered, in a 350° oven for 20 minutes. Uncover and bake 15 minutes more. Serves 6.

Turkey-Rice Amandine

2 cups chicken broth
⅔ cup long grain rice
2 tablespoons butter *or* margarine
3 tablespoons all-purpose flour
½ teaspoon salt
¼ teaspoon dry mustard
⅛ teaspoon pepper
2 cups milk
1 cup shredded sharp cheddar cheese
1 10-ounce package frozen cut broccoli,
      cooked and well drained
2½ cups chopped cooked turkey
⅓ cup fine dry bread crumbs
⅓ cup toasted, slivered almonds
1 to 2 tablespoons butter *or* margarine,
      melted

In saucepan bring the chicken broth and uncooked rice to boiling. Reduce heat; cook, covered, for 15 minutes. Remove from heat; let the rice stand covered for 10 minutes.

Meanwhile, for cheese sauce melt the 2 tablespoons butter or margarine in a saucepan. Stir in the flour, salt, mustard, and pepper. Add milk all at once; cook and stir till thickened and bubbly. Stir in cheese; continue cooking and stirring till cheese is melted. Set aside. Spread drained broccoli in the bottom of a 10x6x2-inch baking dish. Over the broccoli spread the cooked rice and the cooked turkey; pour cheese sauce over all. Combine bread crumbs, almonds, and the 1 to 2 tablespoons melted butter or margarine; toss to mix. Sprinkle over all. Bake in a 350° oven for 20 minutes or till bubbly at edges. Makes 6 servings.

Buying Guide for Cooked Chicken

As a rule-of-thumb, two whole raw chicken breasts (10 ounces each) yield about 2 cups chopped or cubed cooked chicken. One uncooked 2½- to 3-pound broiler-fryer chicken yields about 2½ cups chopped cooked meat, and a 3½-pound roasting chicken provides about 3 cups cooked meat for use in recipes.

Chicken Breasts with Wild Rice

1 teaspoon finely shredded orange peel
⅓ cup orange juice
⅓ cup raisins
3 whole small chicken breasts, halved lengthwise
3 tablespoons butter *or* margarine
1 14½-ounce can chicken broth
2 tablespoons sliced green onion
⅓ cup wild rice, rinsed
⅔ cup long grain rice
2 cups small broccoli flowerets
1 3-ounce can sliced mushrooms, drained
2 tablespoons snipped parsley

Set peel aside. Combine orange juice and raisins; set aside. In 12-inch skillet brown chicken in butter. Sprinkle with salt. Remove chicken and set aside. Stir broth, onion, and peel into skillet; bring to boiling. Stir in uncooked wild rice; return to boiling. Return chicken to skillet. Reduce heat; cover and simmer 25 minutes. Stir in uncooked long grain rice and raisin mixture; cover and simmer 20 minutes more. Stir in remaining ingredients. Cover; cook 10 minutes or till broccoli is crisptender. Serves 6.

Chicken and Stuffing Scallop

½ cup chopped onion
½ cup chopped celery *or* carrot
¼ cup butter *or* margarine
1 8-ounce package herb-seasoned stuffing mix *or* croutons
2 6¾-ounce cans chunk chicken, flaked
2 apples, peeled, cored, and chopped
½ cup chopped nuts
2 beaten eggs
1½ cups chicken broth, apple juice, *or* water
1½ cups shredded cheddar, Monterey Jack, Swiss, *or* American cheese (6 ounces)

In skillet cook onion and celery or carrot in butter till tender. In bowl combine stuffing mix, chicken, apples, and nuts. Add onion mixture and eggs. Add enough of the 1½ cups liquid to thoroughly moisten. Toss lightly and turn into a 12x7½x2-inch baking dish. Bake in a 350° oven for 30 to 40 minutes or till lightly browned. Sprinkle cheese atop; bake 2 minutes more. Serves 6.

Chicken-Broccoli Puff

1 10-ounce package frozen chopped broccoli
3 tablespoons butter *or* margarine
2 tablespoons all-purpose flour
1 teaspoon poultry seasoning
½ teaspoon salt
1 cup milk
½ cup shredded cheddar cheese (2 ounces)
2½ cups cubed cooked chicken
1 tablespoon chopped pimiento
___

3 egg yolks
⅛ teaspoon salt
1 teaspoon finely chopped green onion
¼ teaspoon celery seed
___

3 egg whites
1 tablespoon grated Parmesan cheese

Cook broccoli according to package directions; drain and set aside. In a saucepan melt butter or margarine; stir in flour, poultry seasoning, and the ½ teaspoon salt. Add milk all at once. Cook and stir till mixture is thickened and bubbly. Stir in the shredded cheddar cheese till melted. Stir in the cooked broccoli, cooked chicken, and the pimiento; heat till bubbly. Cover the mixture and keep warm.

In small mixer bowl beat egg yolks and the ⅛ teaspoon salt about 4 minutes or till thick and lemon colored. Add green onion and celery seed. Wash beaters thoroughly.

Beat egg whites till stiff peaks form (tips stand straight). Fold egg yolk mixture into egg whites. Spoon hot chicken mixture into the bottom of an ungreased 9-inch quiche dish or 8x1½-inch round baking dish. Spread egg mixture over hot chicken mixture. Sprinkle grated Parmesan cheese atop. Bake in a 350° oven about 30 minutes or till the egg mixture is golden brown. Serve the puff immediately. Makes 6 servings.

Chicken-Artichoke Casseroles

1 9-ounce package frozen artichoke hearts
2 cups cubed cooked chicken
2 tablespoons butter *or* margarine
2 tablespoons all-purpose flour
1 teaspoon instant chicken bouillon
   granules
½ teaspoon dried savory, crushed
½ teaspoon dried thyme, crushed
¼ teaspoon pepper
⅛ teaspoon ground nutmeg
1¼ cups milk
1½ cups shredded cheddar cheese
   (6 ounces)
¼ cup fine dry bread crumbs
1 tablespoon butter *or* margarine, melted

Cook artichoke hearts according to package directions; drain well. Halve any large pieces of artichoke. Arrange artichokes in 4 individual casseroles. Divide cubed chicken among the 4 casseroles, placing atop the artichoke hearts.

In medium saucepan melt the 2 tablespoons butter or margarine. Stir in the flour, chicken bouillon granules, savory, thyme, pepper, and nutmeg. Add milk all at once. Cook and stir till mixture is slightly thickened and bubbly. Stir in the cheese till melted. Pour the sauce over chicken and artichokes in casseroles.

Combine the bread crumbs and the 1 tablespoon melted butter or margarine. Sprinkle atop casseroles. Bake in a 350° oven about 15 minutes or till heated through. Makes 4 servings.

For a luncheon, serve these individual casseroles with a fruit salad & freshly baked rolls.

Curried Chicken Bake

1½ cups sliced fresh mushrooms
¼ cup chopped onion
1½ teaspoons curry powder
1 clove garlic, minced
¼ cup butter *or* margarine
¼ cup all-purpose flour
1 13-ounce can evaporated milk
½ cup chicken broth
2 cups chopped cooked chicken
½ of a 24-ounce package (2 cups) frozen
   crinkle-cut sliced carrots, cooked and
   drained
½ cup chopped peanuts
1 3-ounce can chow mein noodles

In large saucepan cook first 4 ingredients in butter till onions are tender. Stir in flour, 1 teaspoon *salt,* and dash *pepper.* Add milk and broth; cook and stir till thickened and bubbly. Add chicken, carrots, and peanuts; mix lightly. Turn into a 10x6x2-inch baking dish. Sprinkle with noodles. Bake in a 350° oven for 25 to 30 minutes or till heated through. Serves 4.

Parmesan Chicken Skillet

¼ cup all-purpose flour
1 teaspoon dried basil, crushed
1 teaspoon dried oregano, crushed
¼ teaspoon garlic powder
2 whole medium chicken breasts, halved
   lengthwise
1 tablespoon lemon juice
2 tablespoons cooking oil
1 16-ounce can tomato wedges
2 cups sliced fresh mushrooms
2 small zucchini, cut into ½-inch slices
⅓ cup grated Parmesan cheese

In paper or plastic bag combine flour, basil, oregano, garlic powder, ¼ teaspoon *salt,* and ¼ teaspoon *pepper.* Brush chicken with lemon juice; add to bag and shake to coat well. In a 10-inch skillet slowly brown chicken in hot oil for 10 to 15 minutes, turning to brown evenly. Add *undrained* tomato wedges. Cover; simmer 30 minutes or till nearly done. Add mushrooms and zucchini; cover and simmer 5 to 10 minutes or till vegetables and chicken are done. Sprinkle with cheese. Makes 4 servings.

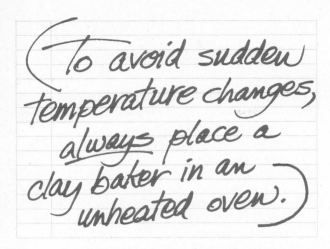

To avoid sudden temperature changes, always place a clay baker in an unheated oven.

Chicken-Noodle Casserole

1 cup sliced fresh mushrooms
¼ cup chopped green pepper
3 tablespoons sliced green onion
2 tablespoons butter *or* margarine
2 cups chopped cooked chicken
1 10¾-ounce can condensed cream of chicken soup
1 cup shredded sharp cheddar cheese (4 ounces)
½ cup dairy sour cream
2 tablespoons chopped pimiento
1 tablespoon snipped parsley
¼ teaspoon celery salt
Dash pepper
4 ounces (3 cups) medium noodles, cooked and drained

⅓ cup fine dry bread crumbs
2 tablespoons grated Parmesan cheese
2 tablespoons butter *or* margarine, melted

In a large saucepan cook mushrooms, green pepper, and green onion in 2 tablespoons butter or margarine till tender. Remove from heat. Stir in the chicken, condensed soup, cheese, sour cream, pimiento, parsley, celery salt, and pepper; blend well. Gently fold in the cooked noodles. Turn into a 2-quart casserole. Combine the bread crumbs, Parmesan cheese, and the 2 tablespoons melted butter or margarine; mix well. Sprinkle crumb mixture atop casserole. Bake in a 350° oven for 45 to 50 minutes or till heated through. Makes 6 servings.

Clay Baker Chicken Rosemary

1 2½- to 3-pound broiler-fryer chicken, cut up
1 tablespoon butter *or* margarine, melted
1 teaspoon dried rosemary, crushed
1 bay leaf, crumbled
½ teaspoon salt
Dash pepper
¼ cup dry white wine

4 medium potatoes, peeled and halved
4 medium carrots, bias cut into 2-inch pieces
12 brussels sprouts
1 small onion, cut into wedges
2 tablespoons snipped parsley

Soak a 2-quart clay baker and upturned lid in water to cover for 10 minutes; drain. Brush chicken pieces with melted butter or margarine and place in baker. Combine rosemary, bay leaf, salt, and pepper; sprinkle over chicken. Pour wine into baker (do not pour over chicken). Arrange potatoes, carrots, brussels sprouts, and onion around chicken and sprinkle with parsley. Cover baker and place in an unheated oven. Turn oven to 450° and bake for 1¼ hours or till chicken and vegetables are tender. Skim fat from juices; spoon juices over chicken and vegetables. Serves 6.

Baking Dishes and Casseroles

A *baking dish* usually is square or rectangular and is shallow. To determine the dimensions of a baking dish, measure across the top from the inside edges. You can use foil when the recipe specifies a cover.

A *casserole* is round or oval-shaped and often has a fitted cover. To determine the volume of the casserole, measure the amount of water it holds when filled completely to the top.

Salmon-Macaroni Pie

1¼ cups elbow macaroni
3 tablespoons butter *or* margarine
2 tablespoons all-purpose flour
½ teaspoon salt
Dash pepper
2 cups milk
¾ cup chopped celery
¼ cup finely chopped onion
2 cups shredded American, cheddar, *or*
  Swiss cheese (8 ounces)

1 15½-ounce can salmon, drained and skin
  and bones removed, *or* one 12½-ounce
  can tuna, drained
¾ cup soft bread crumbs (1 slice)
2 beaten eggs
1 medium tomato, sliced
Salt
3 slices American cheese, halved
  diagonally

Cook the elbow macaroni in a large amount of boiling salted water till tender. Drain the macaroni and set aside.

In a saucepan melt the butter or margarine; stir in the all-purpose flour, the salt, and pepper. Add milk all at once. Cook and stir until mixture is thickened and bubbly. Stir in the chopped celery, chopped onion, and shredded cheese; stir until the cheese is melted.

Combine the cheese sauce and the drained macaroni. Break salmon or tuna into chunks. Combine macaroni-cheese mixture, salmon or tuna, soft bread crumbs, and beaten eggs. Turn mixture into a greased 12x7½x2-inch baking dish. Bake in a 350° oven for 20 minutes.

Sprinkle tomato slices with salt. Arrange the tomato slices and American cheese triangles atop the macaroni mixture in baking dish. Return to oven. Bake 10 minutes more or till the cheese triangles melt and the tomato slices are heated through. Makes 6 servings.

Salmon-Vegetable Bake

1 10¾-ounce can condensed cream of
  celery soup
1 cup milk

1 15½-ounce can salmon, drained and skin
  and bones removed
1 cup quick-cooking rice
1 cup cubed brick, Monterey Jack, or
  mozzarella cheese (4 ounces)
1 10-ounce package frozen mixed
  vegetables, cooked and drained
½ cup sliced water chestnuts
2 tablespoons chopped pimiento
½ of a 3-ounce can French-fried onions

In a 2-quart casserole combine the condensed cream of celery soup and the milk; mix well. Break the canned salmon into large pieces. Add salmon to the soup-milk mixture in casserole along with the uncooked rice, the cubed cheese, drained mixed vegetables, sliced water chestnuts, and chopped pimiento. Mix well.

Bake the casserole, covered, in a 350° oven for 35 to 40 minutes or till mixture is heated through. Sprinkle French-fried onions atop the salmon mixture. Bake the casserole, uncovered, 5 minutes more or till onions are heated through. Makes 6 servings.

Microwave cooking directions: In a 2-quart nonmetal casserole combine the condensed soup and the milk; mix well. Cook in counter-top microwave oven on high power about 5 minutes or till boiling, stirring once. Stir in the uncooked rice. Cover and let stand 5 minutes.

Break the canned salmon into large pieces. Add to the soup-rice mixture in casserole along with the cubed cheese, drained mixed vegetables, water chestnuts, and pimiento.

Micro-cook, uncovered, on high power 9 minutes or till heated through, stirring once. Top with the French-fried onions. Micro-cook, uncovered, 1 minute more.

Orange-Poached Fish

1 cup orange juice
2 tablespoons dry sherry
1 tablespoon soy sauce
¼ teaspoon salt
   Dash pepper
4 medium carrots, thinly sliced
   (2 cups)
1 medium onion, sliced and separated into
   rings
1 medium green pepper, cut into strips
   (¾ cup)
1 pound frozen flounder *or* sole fillets,
   thawed
¼ cup cold water
2 teaspoons cornstarch
1 medium tomato, cut into eight wedges

In a 12-inch skillet combine orange juice, sherry, soy sauce, salt, and pepper. Add carrots and onion; bring to boiling. Reduce heat; simmer, covered, for 8 minutes or till vegetables are crisp-tender. Stir in green pepper. Push the vegetables to edges of skillet.

Season fish with salt; arrange in center of skillet. Bring to boiling; reduce heat and simmer, covered, 2 to 3 minutes or till fish flakes easily when tested with a fork. Remove fish from skillet; set the fish aside. Combine the cold water and cornstarch; stir into mixture in skillet. Cook and stir till thickened and bubbly; cook and stir 1 to 2 minutes more. Return fish to skillet; arrange tomato wedges atop. Heat through; serve immediately.

If desired, garnish with green onion brushes. Makes 4 servings.

Thawing Frozen Fish

To thaw frozen fish, leave it in its original wrapping and place on a plate in the refrigerator. A 16-ounce package takes about 24 hours to thaw.

For faster thawing, place the wrapped package of fish in *cold* water and change water frequently. A 16-ounce package takes about two hours to thaw with this method. Use thawed fish within a day.

Do not thaw fish at room temperature and *do not* use warm water for thawing, as these methods may cause spoilage.

Fish and Potato Sauté

2 medium potatoes, thinly sliced
2 medium carrots, cut into julienne strips
1 small onion, thinly sliced and separated into rings
¼ teaspoon salt
¼ teaspoon garlic powder
¼ teaspoon dry mustard
¼ teaspoon celery seed
2 tablespoons butter *or* margarine
1 tablespoon cooking oil
1 16-ounce package frozen haddock, flounder, *or* perch fillets, thawed, separated, and cut into 2-inch pieces
2 tablespoons snipped parsley

In a 10-inch skillet cook vegetables in a small amount of water, covered, about 10 minutes or just till tender; drain. Combine salt, garlic powder, mustard, celery seed, and dash *pepper.* Add butter or margarine to vegetables in skillet; sprinkle with salt mixture. Toss gently till the butter is melted and vegetables are coated. Remove vegetables to platter; keep warm.

Add cooking oil to the hot skillet; add fish pieces to hot oil. Cook, uncovered, over medium-high heat 5 to 10 minutes or till fish flakes easily when tested with a fork; turn fish once during cooking. Arrange fish on platter with vegetables; sprinkle with parsley. Makes 4 servings.

Flounder Florentine Skillet

2 tablespoons chopped onion
1 clove garlic, minced
2 tablespoons butter *or* margarine
1 10-ounce package frozen chopped spinach
⅛ teaspoon pepper
⅛ teaspoon ground nutmeg

1 cup sliced fresh mushrooms
2 tablespoons butter *or* margarine
½ cup chicken broth
2 tablespoons dry white wine
1 teaspoon Worcestershire sauce
1 16-ounce package frozen flounder fillets, thawed and separated
1 cup dairy sour cream
2 tablespoons all-purpose flour
3 tablespoons grated Parmesan cheese

In a medium saucepan cook onion and garlic in 2 tablespoons butter or margarine till onion is tender. Place frozen spinach block atop onion mixture. Cook, covered, over very low heat till spinach is thawed, turning the block 2 or 3 times and breaking up spinach. Stir in pepper and nutmeg. Continue cooking 3 to 5 minutes or till spinach is tender. Drain. Set aside and keep warm.

In a 10-inch skillet cook mushrooms in the 2 tablespoons butter or margarine till tender. Stir in chicken broth, wine, and Worcestershire sauce. Arrange fish fillets in the skillet. Bring to boiling; reduce heat. Cover and simmer for 5 minutes or till fish flakes easily when tested with a fork. Gently remove fish fillets.

Stir together the sour cream and flour. Stir into mixture in skillet. Cook and stir over medium heat till thickened and bubbly. Return cooked fillets to sauce, spooning sauce over. Arrange warm spinach mixture around edge of skillet. Sprinkle Parmesan cheese over all. Place 3 inches from heat under broiler for 1 to 2 minutes or till browned. Makes 4 servings.

Fish and Rice Bake

1 16-ounce package frozen sole fillets
2 cups chicken broth
⅔ cup long grain rice
1 10-ounce package frozen chopped
   broccoli, cooked and drained
¼ teaspoon salt
¼ teaspoon dried thyme, crushed
2 tablespoons butter *or* margarine, melted
2 tablespoons snipped parsley
1 tablespoon lemon juice
   Lemon wedges

Unwrap fish and place at room temperature for 20 minutes; cut partially frozen block of fish into 8 pieces. Meanwhile, in saucepan bring chicken broth and rice to boiling; reduce heat. Cook, covered, for 15 minutes. Remove from heat and let stand, covered, for 10 minutes. Stir in cooked broccoli, salt, and thyme. Spoon hot rice mixture into a 10x6x2-inch baking dish. Place fish atop rice and press lightly into rice; sprinkle each piece of fish with a little salt and pepper. Combine butter, parsley, and lemon juice; drizzle over fish. Bake, covered, in a 450° oven for 40 minutes or till fish flakes easily with a fork. Serve with lemon wedges. Makes 4 servings.

Savory Fish Roll-Ups

1 10¾-ounce can condensed cream
   of chicken soup
½ cup dairy sour cream
½ cup milk
½ teaspoon dry mustard
1 10-ounce package frozen chopped
   spinach, thawed and well drained
1 cup herb-seasoned stuffing mix
½ cup shredded carrot
¼ cup butter *or* margarine, melted
2 tablespoons sliced green onion
1 16-ounce package frozen sole fillets,
   thawed and separated
   Paprika

In a medium bowl combine soup, sour cream, milk, and dry mustard; blend well and set aside. In another bowl combine spinach, stuffing mix, carrot, butter or margarine, and green onion. Stir in ¼ *cup* of the soup mixture. Blot fish dry with paper toweling. Place about 2 *tablespoons* stuffing mixture on short side of each fillet; roll up jelly-roll style. Press remaining stuffing mixture into a 10x6x2-inch baking dish. Spoon 1 *cup* of the soup mixture over stuffing. Arrange fish fillets in baking dish; pour remaining soup mixture over all. Bake, covered, in a 350° oven for 20 minutes. Uncover and bake 20 minutes more or till fish flakes easily when tested with a fork. Sprinkle with paprika. Makes 4 servings.

Crispy Fish Fillet Bake

1 10-ounce package frozen chopped
   broccoli
2 tablespoons butter *or* margarine
2 tablespoons all-purpose flour
1 cup milk
1 beaten egg
2 cups cooked rice
2 tablespoons dry white wine
½ teaspoon dried dillweed

1 16-ounce package frozen fish fillets,
   thawed and separated
1 cup coarsely crushed crisp rice cereal
¼ cup sliced almonds
2 tablespoons snipped parsley
2 tablespoons butter *or* margarine, melted
   Lemon slices

Cook broccoli according to package directions; drain and set aside. In a saucepan melt 2 tablespoons butter or margarine; stir in flour, blending well. Add milk; cook and stir till mixture is thickened and bubbly.

Gradually stir *half* of the hot mixture into the beaten egg; mix well. Return all to saucepan. Stir in the cooked broccoli, cooked rice, wine, and dillweed. Turn mixture into a 10x6x2-inch baking dish; set aside.

Sprinkle fish lightly with salt and pepper. Fold fillets in half and place atop rice mixture. Combine crushed cereal, almonds, parsley, and 2 tablespoons melted butter or margarine. Sprinkle over top of fish and rice mixture. Bake in a 350° oven for 45 to 50 minutes or till fish flakes easily when tested with a fork. Garnish with lemon slices. Serves 4.

Scallops Tetrazzini

¾ pound fresh *or* frozen scallops
1½ cups water
1 tablespoon lemon juice
¼ teaspoon salt
1 bay leaf

2 tablespoons sliced green onion
3 tablespoons butter *or* margarine
¼ cup all-purpose flour
¾ teaspoon salt
½ teaspoon dry mustard
⅛ teaspoon pepper
1 cup milk
1 3-ounce can sliced mushrooms, drained
2 tablespoons dry sherry
4 ounces vermicelli, broken
¼ cup grated Parmesan cheese
   Green onions, sliced (optional)

Thaw scallops, if frozen. In saucepan combine scallops, water, lemon juice, salt, and bay leaf. Bring to boiling; reduce heat. Simmer 2 to 3 minutes. Remove scallops and cool; slice. Discard bay leaf; reserve ½ cup of the cooking liquid.

For sauce, in a saucepan cook the 2 tablespoons green onion in butter or margarine till tender. Stir in flour, salt, dry mustard, and pepper. Stir in the milk and the reserved cooking liquid. Cook and stir till thickened and bubbly. Cook and stir 1 to 2 minutes more. Stir in the mushrooms, sherry, and scallops.

Cook vermicelli according to package directions; drain. Spoon hot cooked vermicelli into a 10x6x2-inch baking dish. Top with scallop mixture; sprinkle with Parmesan cheese. Bake in a 350° oven about 20 minutes. Garnish with sliced green onions, if desired. Makes 4 servings.

Pass spiced crab apples or apple rings as a colorful accompaniment for the scallop casserole.

Tuna-Potato Bake

1 10¾-ounce can condensed cream of onion soup
½ cup mayonnaise *or* salad dressing
½ cup dairy sour cream
¼ teaspoon garlic powder
¼ teaspoon dried dillweed
2 6½-ounce cans tuna, drained and flaked
1 10-ounce package frozen chopped spinach, thawed and well drained
1 8-ounce can whole kernel corn, drained
½ cup chopped celery
1 16-ounce package frozen fried potato nuggets

In a bowl combine condensed soup, mayonnaise or salad dressing, sour cream, garlic powder, and dillweed; mix well. Gently stir in tuna, drained spinach, corn, and celery. Turn into a 12x7½x2-inch baking dish. Top with potato nuggets. Bake in a 350° oven about 45 minutes. Let stand 5 minutes before serving. Makes 6 servings.

Puff-Top Tuna Casserole

1 9-ounce package frozen Italian green beans *or* cut green beans
1 10¾-ounce can condensed tomato soup
½ cup water
1 tablespoon minced dried onion
1 tablespoon soy sauce
1 teaspoon lemon juice
2 6½-ounce cans tuna, drained and flaked
¾ cup dairy sour cream
2 tablespoons diced pimiento
¼ teaspoon garlic powder
1¼ cups packaged biscuit mix

Cook Italian or cut green beans according to package directions; drain and set aside.

In a 10-inch oven-going skillet stir together beans, condensed soup, water, onion, soy sauce, and lemon juice. Cook, covered, over low heat till heated through. Stir in tuna; return to boiling.

Meanwhile, prepare drop biscuits by combining sour cream, pimiento, and garlic powder; mix well. Add biscuit mix, stirring just till combined. Drop biscuits by tablespoonfuls onto hot tuna mixture. Bake in a 425° oven about 25 minutes or till biscuits are golden brown. Makes 6 servings.

Tuna-Broccoli Bake

1 10¾-ounce can condensed cream of
  chicken soup
½ cup dairy sour cream
1 cup shredded American cheese
¼ teaspoon garlic powder
4 ounces rotini, cooked and drained
½ cup sliced water chestnuts
¼ cup chopped green pepper
2 tablespoons chopped pimiento
1 6½-ounce can tuna, drained and flaked
1 10-ounce package frozen cut broccoli,
  cooked and drained

In a small bowl combine condensed soup, sour cream, ½ *cup* of the cheese, and the garlic powder; mix well. Fold in rotini or elbow macaroni, water chestnuts, green pepper, and pimiento. Gently fold in tuna. Turn into an 8x8x2-inch baking dish; top with cooked broccoli. Sprinkle remaining ½ cup shredded cheese atop. Bake in a 375° oven for 25 to 30 minutes or till bubbly around edges. Makes 5 servings.

Gourmet Crab Casseroles

2 10-ounce packages frozen cut asparagus
½ cup mayonnaise *or* salad dressing
½ cup dairy sour cream
1 teaspoon Worcestershire sauce
1 teaspoon prepared mustard
  Dash ground red pepper
2 7-ounce cans crab meat, drained, flaked,
  and cartilage removed
3 hard-cooked eggs, chopped
¾ cup soft bread crumbs (1 slice)
¼ cup slivered almonds
½ teaspoon dried savory, crushed
3 tablespoons butter *or* margarine, melted

Cook asparagus according to package directions; drain and set aside. In a medium bowl stir together mayonnaise, sour cream, Worcestershire, mustard, and red pepper. Fold in asparagus, crab, and eggs. Turn into 6 individual casseroles. Combine soft bread crumbs, almonds, and savory; toss with melted butter. Sprinkle bread crumb mixture atop casseroles. Bake in a 400° oven for 25 to 30 minutes or till topping is golden and mixture is heated through. Makes 6 servings.

43

Shrimp Casserole

1 10¾-ounce can condensed cream of
  chicken soup
1 cup dairy sour cream
2 beaten egg yolks
2 6-ounce packages frozen cooked
  shrimp, thawed and drained
1 9-ounce package frozen Italian green
  beans, cooked and drained
½ of an 8-ounce can (½ cup) sliced water
  chestnuts, drained
½ cup chopped salted cashews
1 2-ounce jar diced pimiento, drained
3 slices white bread, cut into triangles
¼ cup butter *or* margarine
¾ cup shredded American cheese
  (3 ounces)
1 tablespoon milk
1 tablespoon sliced green onion
2 egg whites

In large saucepan combine the condensed soup and sour cream; heat through over medium heat, stirring constantly. Stir about *1 cup* of the hot mixture into beaten yolks; return all to saucepan. Add shrimp, cooked green beans, water chestnuts, cashews, and pimiento; heat through. Turn into a 12x7½x2-inch baking dish. Arrange the bread triangles atop.

In a small saucepan melt butter; add cheese, milk, and green onion. Stir over low heat till cheese melts. Beat egg whites till stiff peaks form; fold in cheese mixture. Pour over bread triangles in casserole. Bake in a 325° oven for 18 to 20 minutes or till golden. Makes 6 servings.

Making Soft Bread Crumbs

Casserole recipes often call for soft bread crumbs. Use your blender to easily prepare the crumbs. Just tear bread slices into quarters and place a few bread quarters at a time in blender container. Cover and blend till coarsely chopped. Or, you can tear bread into crumbs by hand. A slice of bread makes about ¾ cup soft bread crumbs.

Mac 'n' Cheese Puff

- ½ cup elbow macaroni
- 2 beaten egg yolks
- 1⅓ cups milk
- 1 tablespoon butter *or* margarine
- 1 tablespoon Dijon-style mustard
- 2 teaspoons minced dried onion
- 1 cup shredded American cheese
- 2 cups soft bread crumbs
- 2 stiff-beaten egg whites
- 8 ounces frankfurters, bias sliced

Cook macaroni in boiling salted water 10 minutes or till tender; drain. In saucepan combine yolks, milk, butter, mustard, onion, ¼ teaspoon *salt*, and dash *pepper*; add cheese. Cook and stir over medium heat about 10 minutes or till mixture thickens slightly (do not boil). Stir in macaroni and crumbs. Fold in egg whites. Pour *half* the mixture into a 1½-quart soufflé dish. Reserve a few sliced franks for the top. Place remaining franks in casserole. Pour on remaining macaroni mixture. Arrange franks atop. Bake in a 350° oven for 45 minutes. Serve at once. Makes 6 servings.

Creamy Asparagus Omelet

- 1 cup frozen loose-pack cut asparagus
- 2 tablespoons finely chopped green pepper
- 1 tablespoon finely chopped onion
- 2 tablespoons butter *or* margarine
- 4 beaten eggs
- ¼ cup dairy sour cream
- ½ teaspoon dried thyme, crushed
- 1 3-ounce package cream cheese, cut into ¼-inch cubes

Cook asparagus according to package directions; keep warm. In 10-inch omelet pan or skillet cook pepper and onion in butter till tender. Lift and tilt pan to coat all sides. Stir together eggs, sour cream, thyme, and ⅛ teaspoon *pepper*. Stir in cheese. Pour mixture into skillet. Cook; as eggs set, run spatula around edge of skillet, lifting eggs to allow uncooked portion to flow underneath. Cook till mixture is almost set. Place under broiler 5 inches from heat for 1 to 2 minutes or just till top is set. Drain asparagus; arrange over omelet. Serve in wedges. Serves 2.

Cheesy Italian Supper Pie

- Pastry
- 5 eggs
- 2 cups ricotta cheese
- 1 cup grated Parmesan cheese
- ¼ cup chopped onion
- 2 tablespoons snipped parsley
- ½ teaspoon salt
- ¼ teaspoon pepper

- 2 cloves garlic, minced
- 1 teaspoon dried oregano, crushed
- ½ teaspoon dried marjoram, crushed
- ⅛ teaspoon salt
- 2 tablespoons olive oil *or* cooking oil
- 1 10½-ounce can tomato puree
- ⅔ cup sliced pitted ripe olives
- 1 8-ounce package sliced mozzarella cheese
- ½ cup sliced fresh mushrooms
- 1 cup sliced green pepper

Prepare Pastry; roll out and line a 10-inch pie plate with *half* the Pastry. Trim edge.

Beat eggs; stir in the ricotta cheese, Parmesan cheese, chopped onion, parsley, ½ teaspoon salt, and the pepper. Set aside.

Cook garlic, oregano, marjoram, and the ⅛ teaspoon salt in hot olive oil or cooking oil for 1 minute. Stir in the tomato puree and olives. Spread *half* the egg mixture in the pastry shell. Top with *half* of the mozzarella cheese, then *half* the tomato mixture. Place *half* the mushrooms and *half* the green pepper slices over the cheese layer. Repeat with egg mixture, mozzarella cheese, tomato mixture, mushrooms, and green pepper.

Roll out remaining Pastry for top crust; cut slits in crust for escape of steam. Place over filling; seal and flute edges. Cover edges with foil. Bake in a 425° oven for 20 minutes. Uncover and bake 25 to 30 minutes more. Makes 6 to 8 servings.

Pastry: In medium mixing bowl stir together 2 cups all-purpose *flour* and 1 teaspoon *salt*. Cut in ⅔ cup *shortening or lard* till pieces are the size of small peas. Using 6 to 7 tablespoons *cold water*, sprinkle 1 tablespoon water at a time over part of the mixture; gently toss with fork. Push to side of bowl. Repeat till all of the mixture is moistened. Form dough into 2 balls.

Egg and Spinach Pie

Pastry (see recipe, page 44)
1¼ pounds fresh spinach *or* Swiss chard,
   or two 10-ounce packages frozen
   chopped spinach
½ cup chopped onion
2 tablespoons cooking oil
½ teaspoon ground nutmeg
9 eggs
1 cup grated Parmesan cheese
1 beaten egg (optional)

Prepare Pastry; roll out and line a 9-inch pie plate with *half* the Pastry. Trim edge. Wash and chop fresh spinach. In Dutch oven cook spinach in a small amount of water, uncovered, till limp. (Or, cook frozen spinach according to package directions, omitting salt.) Drain; squeeze out excess liquid. Cook onion in hot oil till tender; stir in nutmeg. Combine *3* of the eggs, the cheese, and onion mixture; stir in spinach. Turn into crust. Make 6 wells in spinach mixture; break one of the remaining eggs into each well.

Roll out remaining Pastry. Place over filling, seal and flute edges. Use any remaining pastry for cutouts, if desired, and arrange atop the crust. If desired, combine the 1 beaten egg and 1 tablespoon *water;* brush atop crust. Cut slits. Bake in a 375° oven for 50 minutes. Let stand 10 minutes before serving. Makes 6 servings.

Blue Cheese and Vegetable Bake

4 ounces medium egg noodles (3 cups)
1 16-ounce can French-style green beans
1 16-ounce can whole kernel corn
½ cup chopped onion
¼ cup butter *or* margarine
¼ cup all-purpose flour
2 cups milk
1 teaspoon prepared mustard
1½ cups shredded sharp cheddar cheese
½ cup crumbled blue cheese
6 hard-cooked eggs, sliced
2 slices bread, cut into ½-inch cubes
2 tablespoons butter, melted

Cook noodles; drain. Drain beans and corn. In saucepan cook onion in the ¼ cup butter till tender. Stir in flour. Add milk and mustard. Cook and stir till thick and bubbly. Cook and stir 1 to 2 minutes more. Stir in cheese till melted. Stir together *2 cups* of the cheese mixture, the noodles, and vegetables. Turn into a 2-quart casserole. Top with egg; pour remaining sauce atop. Combine bread and 2 tablespoons butter; sprinkle atop. Bake in 350° oven 45 to 50 minutes. Serves 6.

Sourdough Cheese Strata

½ of a 16-ounce loaf unsliced sourdough bread *or* French bread
2 cups shredded Monterey Jack cheese
½ cup grated Parmesan cheese
¼ cup chopped onion
3 eggs
2 cups milk
2 tablespoons snipped parsley
2 teaspoons prepared mustard

Cut bread into 1-inch slices. Arrange *half* the bread in greased 9x9x2-inch baking pan. Sprinkle both cheeses over bread. Top with remaining bread. Cook onion in small amount of boiling water about 5 minutes or till tender; drain. In a mixer bowl beat together eggs, milk, parsley, mustard, onion, ¼ teaspoon *salt,* and ⅛ teaspoon *pepper;* slowly pour over bread in dish. Cover; refrigerate at least 1 hour. Bake, covered, in a 350° oven for 30 minutes. Uncover; bake 20 to 25 minutes more or till puffy and lightly browned. Let stand 10 minutes before serving. Serves 6.

Deviled Egg Casserole

6 eggs
¼ cup mayonnaise *or* salad dressing
1 teaspoon prepared mustard
⅛ teaspoon salt
Dash pepper

2 cups chicken broth
1 cup long grain rice
½ cup chopped celery
3 tablespoons butter *or* margarine
3 tablespoons all-purpose flour
½ teaspoon salt
Dash pepper
1¾ cups milk
1 cup shredded sharp cheddar cheese (4 ounces)
1 cup diced fully cooked ham
Paprika

For deviled eggs, place the eggs in a saucepan and cover with cold water. Rapidly bring to boiling. When water boils, reduce heat and keep water just below simmering. Cover and cook eggs for 15 to 20 minutes. Cool in cold water; remove shells. Halve lengthwise; remove and mash the egg yolks. Combine mashed yolks with the mayonnaise or salad dressing, prepared mustard, the ⅛ teaspoon salt, and dash pepper. Refill egg whites with the yolk mixture; set aside.

In a saucepan bring chicken broth to boiling. Add uncooked rice and celery; return to boiling. Reduce heat; cook, covered, for 15 minutes. Meanwhile, prepare cheese sauce. In medium saucepan melt butter or margarine; stir in flour, the ½ teaspoon salt, and dash pepper. Add milk all at once; cook and stir till thickened and bubbly. Cook and stir 1 to 2 minutes more. Stir in cheese and heat till melted; set aside.

Stir ham and *1 cup* of the cheese sauce into the rice. Turn into a 12x7½x2-inch baking dish. Arrange the deviled eggs atop rice mixture, pressing each lightly into rice mixture. Sprinkle with paprika. Bake, covered, in a 350° oven for 25 to 30 minutes or till heated through. Makes 6 servings.

Simple Garnishes

Add simple, decorative trims to your casseroles by garnishing them with reserved cooked vegetables from the casserole. Or, for a bit of difference, trim with vegetables not in the dish. Olive or mushroom slices and pimiento strips can be arranged easily and attractively atop a casserole. Other excellent trims are parsley sprigs, a wreath of snipped parsley, green pepper or onion rings, and canned French fried onions.

Hash Brown Ham 'n' Egg Bake

2 cups frozen shredded hash brown
   potatoes, thawed
1 beaten egg
2 tablespoons butter *or* margarine, melted
1 10¾-ounce can condensed cream of
   chicken soup
¼ cup milk
3 tablespoons sliced green onion
½ teaspoon dried basil, crushed
½ teaspoon prepared mustard

8 eggs
1 cup finely chopped fully cooked ham
½ cup fine dry bread crumbs
2 tablespoons butter *or* margarine

For individual crusts, combine potatoes, egg, and the 2 tablespoons melted butter or margarine; mix well. Press into 4 greased individual au gratin dishes. Bake in a 400° oven for 20 to 25 minutes or till lightly browned at edges.

Meanwhile, stir together condensed soup, milk, green onion, basil, and mustard; mix well. Break 2 eggs, one at a time, into each crust. Pour *one-fourth* of the soup mixture evenly around (not over) egg yolks in each dish. Combine ham, bread crumbs, and 2 tablespoons butter; toss to mix. Sprinkle *one-fourth* of the ham mixture over eggs in each dish. Return to oven and bake 20 minutes more or till eggs are desired doneness. Let stand 5 minutes before serving. Makes 4 servings.

Ham and Egg Casserole

1 cup diced fully cooked ham
1 cup sliced fresh mushrooms
¼ cup chopped green pepper
1 clove garlic, minced
1 tablespoon butter *or* margarine
6 beaten eggs
⅓ cup milk

1 tablespoon butter *or* margarine
1 tablespoon all-purpose flour
   Dash pepper
¾ cup milk
½ cup shredded process Swiss cheese
   (2 ounces)
2 tablespoons diced pimiento

¾ cup soft bread crumbs (1 slice)
2 tablespoons butter *or* margarine, melted
1 tablespoon grated Parmesan cheese
¼ teaspoon dried basil, crushed

In a 10-inch skillet cook ham, mushrooms, green pepper, and garlic in the 1 tablespoon butter or margarine till mushrooms and green pepper are tender. Combine eggs and ⅓ cup milk; add to skillet. Cook without stirring till mixture begins to set on bottom and around edges. As eggs set, run a spatula around edge of skillet, lifting the eggs to allow uncooked portion to flow underneath. Continue cooking till mixture is set. Remove from heat and set aside.

In saucepan melt the 1 tablespoon butter or margarine; blend in flour and pepper. Add ¾ cup milk; cook and stir till mixture is slightly thickened and bubbly. Cook and stir 1 to 2 minutes more. Add cheese and pimiento; cook and stir till cheese is melted. Add to cooked eggs; fold together. Turn into a 10x6x2-inch baking dish. In a bowl combine the bread crumbs, 2 tablespoons melted butter or margarine, the Parmesan cheese, and basil; toss well. Sprinkle atop casserole. Bake in a 350° oven for 15 to 20 minutes. Makes 4 servings.

Freezing Basics

A benefit of many one-dish meals is that they can be prepared and stored in the freezer. When preparing a one-dish meal, make extra to freeze for later use. Then, on a busy day just choose from your prepared-ahead selection of homemade casseroles, skillet meals, soups, stews, and sandwiches. To ensure the quality of frozen one-dish meals, follow these few guidelines. Start with high-quality ingredients, because quality and flavor do not improve with freezing. Observe strict sanitary procedures when preparing food to be frozen. Remember, freezer temperatures of 0° F or below merely stop the multiplication of bacteria, but do not kill it. Most casseroles should be frozen before baking, especially when all the ingredients are already cooked. Exceptions to this are dishes that contain uncooked rice, raw vegetables, or uncooked meat that has been frozen and thawed. If a casserole or other one-dish meal is cooked, before freezing it chill it quickly by placing the container in ice water to cool to room temperature. It is best to slightly undercook the food, since it will be reheated later. Avoid freezing certain foods because of the texture and flavor changes that occur (see chart, page 50). Packaging is important

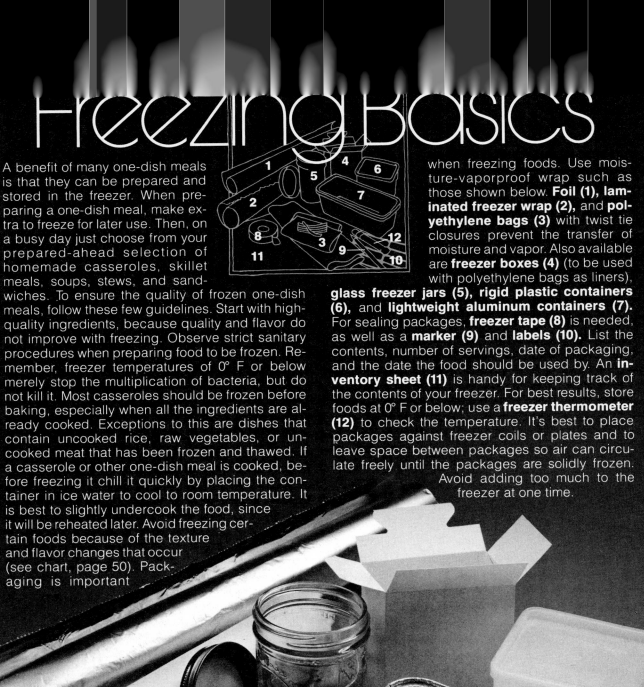

when freezing foods. Use moisture-vaporproof wrap such as those shown below. **Foil (1), laminated freezer wrap (2),** and **polyethylene bags (3)** with twist tie closures prevent the transfer of moisture and vapor. Also available are **freezer boxes (4)** (to be used with polyethylene bags as liners), **glass freezer jars (5), rigid plastic containers (6),** and **lightweight aluminum containers (7).** For sealing packages, **freezer tape (8)** is needed, as well as a **marker (9)** and **labels (10).** List the contents, number of servings, date of packaging, and the date the food should be used by. An **inventory sheet (11)** is handy for keeping track of the contents of your freezer. For best results, store foods at 0° F or below; use a **freezer thermometer (12)** to check the temperature. It's best to place packages against freezer coils or plates and to leave space between packages so air can circulate freely until the packages are solidly frozen. Avoid adding too much to the freezer at one time.

Proper packaging & wrapping

Be sure one-dish meals are wrapped carefully and in moisture-proof and vapor-proof packaging before freezing in order to prevent loss of moisture. Air allowed to remain in packaged food absorbs moisture from the food and forms a frost. Odors of the food are given off by the frost, which results in off flavors that can be picked up by foods in the freezer. Freezer burn, a grayish-white discoloration on the food surface, is caused by moisture loss that results from improper packaging. Good packaging materials must resist the passage of moisture and vapor, exclude air, be odorless and tasteless, and have the ability to withstand handling at low temperatures. Freezer paper laminated with polyethylene, heavy-duty foil, and polyethylene films and bags are good materials for packaging. Seal the foods by using a special freezer tape with an adhesive that holds at low temperatures. Specially tempered freezing jars are especially good for freezing foods such as soups and stews. (Fill jars to within 1-inch of the top to allow for expansion.) Plastic freezer containers, available in several sizes, are a good choice for freezing food that is cool when poured into the container; tape lids on with freezer tape.

Casserole Wrap

Place the food mixture to be frozen into a casserole or a baking dish lined with foil.

Bring opposite sides of foil together and fold the edges down in a series of locked folds.

Press out air, creasing the ends into points; fold ends to center. Seal with freezer tape; freeze.

When frozen solid, lift from casserole; return to freezer. To serve, remove foil and return to original casserole to heat.

Freezer Wrap

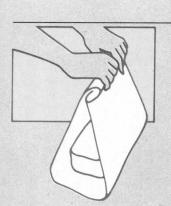

Place food in center of wrap and bring opposite sides together.

Fold edges down in a series of locked folds.

Press the wrap tightly against the food, pressing out air and creasing ends into points.

Fold ends up snugly to center of package; seal with freezer tape.

Freezing Guide for Cooked Foods

FOOD	PREPARATION FOR FREEZING	HOW TO SERVE	STORAGE TIME
Casseroles Meat, fish, or poultry with pasta or vegetables	Prepare slightly undercooked and season lightly; add more seasoning when reheating, if desired. Cool mixture quickly. Turn into freezer-to-oven casserole dish. (Or line dish with foil; see page 49.) Cover or wrap tightly. Seal; label.	Bake, covered, in a 400° oven for half of baking time; uncover for second half of baking time. Allow 1¾ hours for one quart.	3 to 6 months
Meatballs with tomato sauce	Cook till done; cool quickly. Ladle into freezer jars or containers, allowing headspace (don't use metal or foil for acidic foods). Seal; label.	Heat in a heavy saucepan over low heat, stirring frequently. Or, defrost overnight in the refrigerator. Heat through.	3 months
Meatloaf Baked or unbaked	Cool baked meatloaf before wrapping. Place baked or unbaked meatloaf in pan. Wrap, seal, and label.	Thaw baked loaf in refrigerator; serve cold. To reheat, unwrap and bake in a 350° oven for 1 hour or till thawed. For unbaked loaf, unwrap and bake in 350° oven for 1½ hours.	1 to 2 months
Meats, Poultry Broiled or fried	Cool; wrap in plastic film. Seal and label.	Thaw in wrapping in refrigerator.	1 to 3 months
Roasted Large pieces	Trim excess fat, but do not cut up. Wrap, seal, and label.	Thaw wrapped in refrigerator; serve cold. To reheat, unwrap and bake in 350° oven for 1 hour.	Poultry and beef—4 to 6 months. Pork—1 to 3 months.
Slices	Cool and package, making sure slices are covered with gravy.	Unwrap and place unthawed in baking pan. Heat, covered, in 350° oven about 1 hour.	Poultry and beef—4 to 6 months. Pork—1 to 3 months.
Pizza	Prepare as recipe directs but do not bake. Cool; wrap, seal, and label.	Unwrap; bake unthawed in 450° oven 15 to 20 minutes.	2 to 4 weeks
Sandwiches	*These freeze well:* Cream cheese, egg, meat and poultry, tuna or salmon, and peanut butter. Spread bread with softened butter; fill. Wrap tightly. *Not recommended:* Lettuce, celery, tomatoes, cucumber, jelly, and mayonnaise.	Thaw sandwiches in wrapping at room temperature about 3 hours.	1 month
Stews and Soups	Select vegetables that freeze well. Omit potatoes. Green pepper and garlic become more intense in flavor. Omit salt and thickening if stew is to be kept longer than 2 months. Do not completely cook vegetables. Cool quickly; turn into freezer container. Cover, seal, label.	Heat from the frozen state in a heavy saucepan over low heat. Separate with a fork during thawing. Do not overcook. Season and thicken heated stew before serving.	6 months
Stuffing	Cool quickly; wrap, seal, and label.	Unwrap; bake, covered, in 350° oven for 20 minutes. Remove cover; bake 10 minutes more.	1 month

One Dish Meals
Hearty Soups & Stews

Featured for you in this chapter are delicious soups and stews based on beef, pork, lamb, poultry, fish and seafood, and cheese. In each recipe, a carefully chosen blend of ingredients combine to produce soups and stews that serve as the mainstay of the meal. All that's needed to complete the menu is warm crusty bread and a tossed salad. Bowls of these soups and stews are good for a satisfying meal anytime.

Easy Vegetable-Cheese Soup

- 2 cups milk
- 1 10¾-ounce can condensed soup
- 2 teaspoons prepared mustard
- ¼ teaspoon garlic powder
- ¼ teaspoon dried marjoram, crushed
- ⅛ teaspoon pepper
- 1 10-ounce package frozen vegetable, thawed and drained
- 2 cups shredded cheese (8 ounces)
  Roast beef, chicken, or tuna
  (see Meat/Fish Options)

In a 2-quart saucepan stir together milk and condensed soup. Stir in prepared mustard, garlic powder, marjoram, and pepper. Bring to boiling, stirring occasionally. Reduce heat to medium. Stir in vegetable, cheese, and desired meat/fish option. Continue cooking and stirring over medium heat about 15 minutes or till cheese melts and mixture is heated through. Makes 6 servings.

Soup Options
cream of potato
cream of onion
cream of celery

Vegetable Options
sliced zucchini
whole kernel corn
chopped broccoli

Cheese Options
cheddar
brick
American

Meat/Fish Options
1 cup diced cooked roast beef
1 6¾-oz. can chunk-style chicken, drained & chopped
1 6½-oz. can tuna, drained & flaked

Create·a·Stew

Meat, Bean, and Vegetable Stew

1 pound dried beans
8 cups cold water
6 cups hot water
2 pounds meat
1 cup chopped onion
1 tablespoon salt
1 teaspoon dried seasoning, crushed
¼ teaspoon pepper
1 10-ounce package frozen whole kernel corn *or* one 16-ounce can whole kernel corn, drained
2 cups cubed or sliced vegetable

In a 5-quart Dutch oven combine beans and the 8 cups cold water. Bring to boiling; reduce heat. Cover and simmer 2 minutes. Remove from heat. Let stand 1 hour. (Or soak beans in water overnight.) *Drain.* In same Dutch oven combine soaked beans, the 6 cups hot water, the desired meat, onion, salt, seasoning, and pepper. Bring to boiling; reduce heat. Cover and simmer 1½ hours or till meat is nearly tender, stirring occasionally. Mash beans slightly, if desired. Stir in corn and desired vegetable. Simmer, covered, 30 to 40 minutes more or till tender. Remove meat; cool just till easily handled. Remove meat from bones and cube meat. Discard bones. Return meat to Dutch oven and heat through. Makes 6 to 8 servings.

Bean Options
navy beans
pinto beans
lima beans
black-eyed peas

Meat Options
beef shank crosscuts
lamb shanks
fresh pork hocks

Seasoning Options
marjoram
sage
thyme
rosemary

Vegetable Options
sliced parsnips
cubed potatoes
sliced carrots
cubed rutabaga

Surprise Dumpling Stew

16 ounces dry pinto beans (2½ cups)
10 cups cold water
10 cups hot water
¼ pound salt pork, diced (1 cup)
1 cup chopped onion
1 clove garlic, minced
1 teaspoon salt
Dash pepper
½ pound ground beef
¼ cup chopped onion
2 teaspoons chili powder
¼ teaspoon salt
Dash pepper

1½ cups yellow cornmeal
¾ cup all-purpose flour
2 teaspoons baking powder
1 teaspoon salt
1 teaspoon sugar

In a Dutch oven combine beans and the 10 cups cold water. Bring to boiling. Reduce heat and simmer, uncovered 2 minutes. Remove from heat. Cover; let stand 1 hour. (Or, add beans to cold water; soak overnight.) Drain and rinse soaked beans; add the 10 cups hot water, the salt pork, the 1 cup chopped onion, the garlic, 1 teaspoon salt, and dash pepper to the beans. Cover and simmer for 2½ hours or till beans are tender. In a skillet cook ground beef and the ¼ cup chopped onion till meat is browned and onion is tender. Drain off excess fat. Season with chili powder, the ¼ teaspoon salt, and dash pepper. Cool meat mixture.

To make cornmeal dumplings remove 1 cup liquid from the beans; set aside to cool slightly. In a bowl combine cornmeal, flour, baking powder, 1 teaspoon salt, and sugar. Add the 1 cup bean liquid, stirring constantly, till well mixed. Divide mixture into 16 portions. With lightly floured hands, shape each portion around *1 teaspoon* of meat mixture to form a ball. Mash beans slightly. Stir any remaining meat filling into beans. Drop dumplings onto simmering beans. Cover tightly; cook 30 minutes. Serve in bowls. Makes 8 servings.

Beef and Cheese Soup

1 pound ground beef
1 medium onion, chopped (½ cup)
1 10-ounce package frozen mixed
   vegetables
½ cup water
1 11½-ounce can condensed bean with
   bacon soup
1 10¾-ounce can condensed tomato soup
1¾ cups milk
1 cup shredded American cheese
   (4 ounces)
1½ teaspoons Worcestershire sauce

In a 3-quart saucepan cook ground beef and onion till meat is browned and onion is tender; drain off fat. Stir in frozen vegetables and water. Cover and cook over medium high heat 10 to 12 minutes or till vegetables are tender. Stir in bean with bacon soup, tomato soup, milk, cheese, and Worcestershire. Cook and stir till cheese is melted and soup is heated through. Makes 6 servings.

Hearty Hamburger Soup

1 pound ground beef
½ medium onion, chopped
4 cups water
1 16-ounce can stewed tomatoes
1 10-ounce package frozen whole
   kernel corn
1 9-ounce package frozen cut green beans
1 cup thinly sliced carrot
3 tablespoons instant beef bouillon
   granules
2 tablespoons snipped parsley
1 teaspoon dried basil, crushed
½ teaspoon dried oregano, crushed
⅛ teaspoon pepper

In a large saucepan or Dutch oven cook ground beef and onion till meat is browned and onion is tender. Drain off excess fat. Stir in water, *undrained* stewed tomatoes, corn, green beans, carrot, bouillon granules, parsley, basil, oregano, and pepper. Bring to boiling; reduce heat. Cover and simmer about 15 minutes, stirring occasionally. Makes 5 or 6 servings.

Burgundy Meat and Bean Stew

16 ounces dry pinto beans (2½ cups)
7 cups cold water
7 cups hot water
1 pound meaty beef bone *or* beef shank crosscuts
¾ pound meaty ham bone *or* smoked pork hock
1 clove garlic, minced
1 bay leaf
1 teaspoon salt
¼ teaspoon pepper
1 16-ounce can tomatoes, cut up
1½ cups burgundy
1 8-ounce can tomato sauce
2 tablespoons packed brown sugar

In a Dutch oven combine beans and the 7 cups cold water. Bring to boiling. Reduce heat and simmer, uncovered, 2 minutes. Remove from heat. Cover and let stand 1 hour. (Or, add beans to cold water; cover and let stand overnight.) Drain and rinse soaked beans; add the 7 cups hot water, the beef bone or crosscuts, ham bone or pork hock, garlic, bay leaf, salt, and pepper. Bring to boiling. Cover; simmer 1½ hours, stirring occasionally. Remove bones; when cool enough to handle, remove meat from bones. Cut up meat and return to stew. Discard bones. Add *undrained* tomatoes, burgundy, tomato sauce, and brown sugar. Simmer, covered, about 45 minutes more or till beans are tender. Remove bay leaf. Mash beans slightly. Season to taste with salt and pepper. Serves 8.

Soaking Dry Beans

Dry beans and dry whole peas need soaking before cooking, but split peas and lentils do not. Rinse and drain all these before cooking.

To soak, combine dry beans or peas with the specified amount of water in a Dutch oven. Bring to boiling. Reduce heat; simmer 2 minutes. Remove from heat. Cover; let stand 1 hour. (Or, soak beans in water overnight.) Discard the water used for soaking, rinse the beans or peas, and cook them in fresh water.

Beef and Sausage Stew

55

4 slices bacon
1 pound beef stew meat, cut into 1-inch cubes
3 medium apples, peeled, cored and chopped
1 large onion, chopped (1 cup)
2 14½-ounce cans beef broth
1 pound Polish Sausage, cut into bite-size pieces
6 medium carrots, sliced (3 cups)
6 cups chopped cabbage
¼ cup all-purpose flour

In a Dutch oven cook bacon till crisp, reserving drippings in pan. Crumble bacon; set aside. Cook beef in bacon drippings till browned. Add apples and onion; reduce heat. Cook, covered, 5 minutes. Reserve ½ *cup* of beef broth; add remaining broth to stew along with 1 teaspoon *salt*. Simmer, covered, 1 hour. Add sausage and carrots; simmer, covered, 30 minutes. Add cabbage; simmer, covered, 10 minutes more. Blend flour and reserved ½ cup beef broth; stir into stew. Cook and stir till thick and bubbly. Cook and stir 1 to 2 minutes more. Top with crumbled bacon. Serves 8.

Veal Shank and Lentil Soup

2 pounds veal shanks
2 tablespoons cooking oil
½ cup chopped onion
⅓ cup snipped parsley
2 tablespoons instant chicken bouillon granules
½ teaspoon celery seed
1 teaspoon dried basil, crushed
½ teaspoon dried rosemary, crushed
10 ounces dry lentils (1½ cups)
3 medium carrots, thinly sliced

Brown shanks in hot oil; drain. Add onion, parsley, bouillon, celery seed, basil, rosemary, 7 cups *water,* ½ teaspoon *salt,* and ¼ teaspoon *pepper.* Bring to boiling; reduce heat. Cover and simmer 30 minutes. Add lentils and carrots; simmer 45 minutes. Remove shanks. When cool enough to handle, remove meat from bones; cut up meat and return to soup. Discard bones. Continue cooking till meat is heated through. Serves 6.

Texts-Style Hot Chili

pictured on page 4

5 slices bacon
8 ounces hot Italian sausage links, sliced
1½ pounds boneless beef chuck shoulder steak, diced
1 cup chopped onion
½ cup chopped green pepper
1 clove garlic, minced
3 cups water
1 12-ounce can tomato paste
1 to 2 dried red chili peppers, seeded and crumbled
1 to 2 jalapeño peppers, seeded and chopped
1 to 1½ tablespoons chili powder
½ teaspoon salt
¼ teaspoon dried oregano, crushed
1 16-ounce can pinto beans, drained

In a 4-quart Dutch oven cook bacon till crisp; drain. Crumble bacon and set aside. In Dutch oven cook sausage till lightly browned. Stir in beef, onion, green pepper, and garlic. Continue cooking till beef is browned; drain off excess fat. Stir in bacon, water, tomato paste, chili peppers, jalapeño peppers, chili powder, salt, and oregano. Bring to boiling; reduce heat. Cover and simmer for 2 hours. Stir in beans. Cover and simmer 20 minutes more or till beans are heated through. Makes 8 servings.

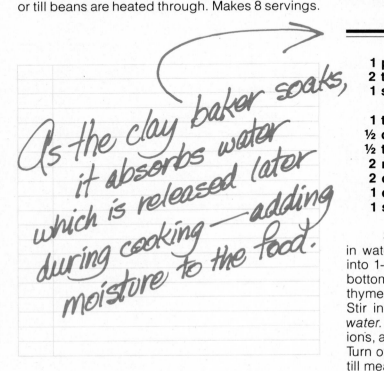

As the clay baker soaks, it absorbs water which is released later during cooking—adding moisture to the food.

Beef and Barley Soup

3 pounds beef shank crosscuts
1 clove garlic, minced
1 tablespoon cooking oil
1 8-ounce can tomatoes, cut up
1 8-ounce can tomato sauce
1 cup dry red wine
1 bay leaf
1 teaspoon dried thyme, crushed
1½ cups sliced carrots
1 stalk celery, sliced
½ cup pearl barley
¼ cup snipped parsley

In a Dutch oven cook beef and garlic in hot oil till beef is browned; drain. Stir in *undrained* tomatoes, tomato sauce, wine, bay leaf, thyme, 6 cups *water,* 1½ teaspoons *salt,* and ¼ teaspoon *pepper.* Bring to boiling; reduce heat. Simmer, covered, for 1 hour. Stir in carrots, celery, and barley. Simmer, uncovered, 1 hour more, stirring occasionally. Remove beef and discard bay leaf; skim off any fat. Cool beef slightly and remove meat from bones; cut up and return to soup. Heat through. Stir in parsley. Makes 6 to 8 servings.

Clay Baker Beef Stew

1 pound beef stew meat
2 tablespoons all-purpose flour
1 single-serving envelope instant tomato soup mix
1 teaspoon dried thyme, crushed
½ cup burgundy
½ teaspoon Worcestershire sauce
2 medium potatoes, peeled and quartered
2 carrots, quartered
1 cup frozen pearl onions
1 stalk celery, sliced

Soak a 2-quart clay baker and upturned lid in water to cover for 10 minutes; drain. Cut beef into 1-inch cubes and coat with flour; arrange in bottom of clay baker. Combine tomato soup mix, thyme, ½ teaspoon *salt,* and ⅛ teaspoon *pepper.* Stir in the burgundy, Worcestershire, and 1 cup *water.* Pour over meat. Add potatoes, carrots, onions, and celery. Cover baker. *Place in a cold oven.* Turn oven to 400° and bake for 1½ to 1¾ hours or till meat and vegetables are tender. Serves 4.

Springtime Beef Stew

¼ cup all-purpose flour
1½ pounds beef stew meat, cut into
    1-inch cubes
3 tablespoons cooking oil *or* olive oil
2 cups beef broth
1 cup dry red wine *or* beef broth
3 tablespoons tomato paste
1 clove garlic, minced
1 bay leaf
1 teaspoon dried thyme, crushed
6 small potatoes, peeled (½ pound)
2 medium carrots, cut into ½-inch pieces
1 medium onion, chopped (½ cup)
1 9-ounce package frozen cut green beans
1 cup shelled peas *or* ½ of 1 10-ounce
    package frozen peas

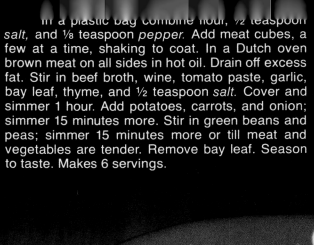

In a plastic bag combine flour, ½ teaspoon *salt,* and ⅛ teaspoon *pepper.* Add meat cubes, a few at a time, shaking to coat. In a Dutch oven brown meat on all sides in hot oil. Drain off excess fat. Stir in beef broth, wine, tomato paste, garlic, bay leaf, thyme, and ½ teaspoon *salt.* Cover and simmer 1 hour. Add potatoes, carrots, and onion; simmer 15 minutes more. Stir in green beans and peas; simmer 15 minutes more or till meat and vegetables are tender. Remove bay leaf. Season to taste. Makes 6 servings.

Calico Pork and Dumpling Stew

2 pounds pork stew meat, cut into 1-inch cubes
2 tablespoons cooking oil
1 28-ounce can tomatoes, cut up
1 12-ounce can beer (1½ cups)
1 medium onion, cut into thin wedges
1 clove garlic, minced
1 tablespoon Worcestershire sauce
1 teaspoon sugar
1 teaspoon dried thyme, crushed
2 bay leaves
¾ teaspoon salt
¼ teaspoon pepper
¼ teaspoon ground nutmeg
1 9-ounce package frozen cut green beans
3 carrots, bias sliced into ½-inch pieces
2 tablespoons all-purpose flour
Cornmeal Dumplings
Paprika (optional)

In a 4-quart Dutch oven brown meat cubes, half at a time, in hot cooking oil. Return all meat to pan. Add *undrained* tomatoes, *1 cup* of the beer, the onion, garlic, Worcestershire sauce, sugar, thyme, bay leaves, salt, pepper, and nutmeg. Bring to boiling; reduce heat. Simmer, covered, 30 minutes. Spoon off fat. Add green beans and carrots; simmer 20 minutes more or till meat and vegetables are tender.

Blend flour and the remaining ½ cup beer together; stir into stew. Cook and stir till thickened and bubbly. Prepare Cornmeal Dumplings. Drop batter by rounded tablespoonfuls onto boiling stew mixture to make 8 dumplings. Sprinkle tops with paprika, if desired. Cover and simmer, *without lifting cover*, 10 to 12 minutes or till dumplings are done. Remove bay leaves. Makes 8 servings.

Cornmeal Dumplings: In bowl stir together ½ cup all-purpose *flour*, ⅓ cup *yellow cornmeal*, 1½ teaspoons *baking powder*, ¼ teaspoon *salt*, and dash *pepper.* Stir together 1 beaten *egg*, ¼ cup *milk,* and 2 tablespoons *cooking oil.* Add to flour mixture and stir just till blended. Stir in ¾ cup shredded *carrot.*

Tofu Soup

1½ cups diced fully cooked ham
1 cup sliced fresh mushrooms
½ of an 8-ounce can bamboo shoots, slivered and drained (½ cup)
½ cup thinly sliced celery
1 tablespoon soy sauce
2 14½-ounce cans chicken broth
8 ounces fresh tofu, finely sliced
3 tablespoons dry sherry
1 green onion, thinly sliced
1 tablespoon cornstarch
1 tablespoon cold water
2 slightly beaten eggs
2 teaspoons sesame oil

In a large saucepan combine ham, mushrooms, bamboo shoots, celery, and soy sauce. Stir in chicken broth. Bring to boiling. Reduce heat and simmer 3 minutes. Season with pepper, if desired. Add tofu, sherry, and green onion; return to boiling. Stir together cornstarch and water; add to soup. Cook and stir till slightly thickened and bubbly. Slowly add beaten eggs to bubbling soup, stirring gently. Remove from heat; stir in oil. Serves 4.

Ham and Garbanzo Soup

2 cups diced fully cooked ham
1 cup chopped onion
1 cup sliced celery
1 clove garlic, minced
1 tablespoon cooking oil
3 cups vegetable juice cocktail
1½ cups water
2 15½-ounce cans garbanzo beans
2 medium potatoes, peeled and diced
1 tablespoon instant beef bouillon granules
½ teaspoon ground allspice
2 bay leaves

In a 4-quart Dutch oven cook ham, onion, celery, and garlic in hot oil till onion is tender but not browned. Stir in vegetable juice cocktail, water, *undrained* garbanzo beans, potatoes, beef bouillon granules, allspice, and bay leaves. Bring to boiling; reduce heat. Cover and simmer about 20 minutes or till potatoes are tender. Remove bay leaves. Makes 6 servings.

Sweet Potato Stew

1½ pounds hot Italian sausage links, cut into 1-inch pieces
4 medium sweet potatoes, peeled and cut into 1-inch cubes (1⅓ pounds)
2 stalks celery, cut into 1-inch pieces (1 cup)
1 medium onion, coarsely chopped (½ cup)
1 16-ounce can tomatoes, cut up
½ cup beef broth
1 15-ounce can garbanzo beans, drained
1 medium green pepper, cut into 1-inch cubes (¾ cup)
1 tablespoon cold water
1 tablespoon cornstarch

In a 4-quart Dutch oven brown sausage pieces. Drain off excess fat. Add sweet potatoes, celery, onion, *undrained* tomatoes, and beef broth. Bring to boiling; reduce heat. Cover and simmer 20 minutes or till vegetables are nearly tender. Add garbanzo beans and green pepper. Cook 5 to 7 minutes more or till tender. Stir together water and cornstarch; stir into stew. Cook and stir till thickened and bubbly. Cook and stir 1 to 2 minutes more. Makes 6 servings.

Cassoulet Chowder

1 cup dry pinto beans
5 cups cold water
5 cups hot water
1 8-ounce package brown-and-serve sausage links, cooked and drained
2 cups cubed fully cooked ham
2 cups cubed cooked chicken
3 medium carrots, sliced (1½ cups)
1 8-ounce can tomato sauce
¾ cup dry red wine
½ cup chopped onion
½ teaspoon garlic powder
½ teaspoon dried thyme, crushed
1 bay leaf

In a 4-quart Dutch oven or large saucepan combine beans and the 5 cups cold water; bring to boiling. Reduce heat; cover and simmer 1½ hours. Drain; stir in the 5 cups hot water, the sausage links, ham, chicken, carrots, tomato sauce,

wine, onion, garlic powder, thyme, and bay leaf. Bring to boiling; reduce heat. Cover and simmer about 45 minutes more. Remove bay leaf. Season chowder to taste with salt and pepper. Makes 8 to 10 servings.

Crockery cooker directions: Prepare beans as above. In a 3½- to 4-quart electric slow crockery cooker combine beans, the 5 cups hot water, and remaining ingredients. Cover and cook on low heat setting for 8 to 10 hours or high heat setting about 4 hours. Remove bay leaf. Season to taste with salt and pepper.

Sausage-Vegetable Soup

1 pound bulk pork sausage
4 cups water
1 15-ounce can great northern beans
1 10-ounce package frozen mixed vegetables
1 8-ounce can tomatoes, cut up
1 cup finely shredded cabbage
2 tablespoons instant beef bouillon granules
½ teaspoon salt
½ teaspoon dried basil, crushed
½ teaspoon dried thyme, crushed
Dash garlic powder
½ cup milk *or* light cream
Grated Parmesan cheese

In a 5-quart Dutch oven cook sausage till browned, stirring occasionally to break sausage into smaller pieces and brown evenly. Drain off fat. Add water, *undrained* beans, frozen mixed vegetables, *undrained* tomatoes, cabbage, bouillon granules, salt, basil, thyme, and garlic powder. Bring to boiling. Reduce heat; simmer, covered, about 20 minutes. Stir in milk or light cream. Sprinkle with Parmesan when served. Makes 6 servings.

Crockery cooker directions: In skillet brown sausage; drain off fat. Transfer to an electric slow crockery cooker. Stir in water, *undrained* beans, frozen mixed vegetables, tomatoes, cabbage, bouillon granules, salt, basil, thyme, and garlic powder. Cover; cook on low heat setting 6 to 8 hours or high heat setting 3 to 4 hours. Skim off any excess fat. Stir in milk or light cream; pass Parmesan when served.

Lamb & fresh vegetables are enhanced by mint and rosemary in this flavorful ragout.

Lamb Ragout

1½ **pounds boneless lamb, cut into**
    ¾-inch cubes
  1 **clove garlic, minced**
  2 **tablespoons cooking oil**
2¼ **cups water**
  1 **small onion, sliced**
  1 **bay leaf**
  1 **teaspoon instant beef bouillon granules**
  1 **teaspoon celery salt**
  ½ **teaspoon mint flakes, crushed**
  ¼ **teaspoon dried rosemary, crushed**
  6 **tiny new potatoes, halved, *or* 3 medium**
    potatoes, peeled and quartered
  3 **medium carrots, cut into 2-inch pieces,**
    ***or* 6 whole small carrots**
  2 **tablespoons butter *or* margarine, melted**
  2 **tablespoons all-purpose flour**

In a Dutch oven, cook lamb and garlic in hot oil till meat is browned. Drain off fat. Add water, onion, bay leaf, beef bouillon granules, celery salt, mint flakes, and rosemary. Bring to boiling; reduce heat. Cover and simmer for 30 minutes. Add potatoes and carrots. Cover and continue cooking about 30 minutes or till lamb and vegetables are tender. Remove bay leaf.

In a small bowl combine melted butter or margarine and flour, blending till smooth. Stir flour mixture into ragout, mixing well. Cook and stir till thickened and bubbly. Makes 6 servings.

Lamb Stew

  ⅓ **cup all-purpose flour**
  ½ **teaspoon salt**
  ½ **teaspoon dried oregano, crushed**
  ⅛ **teaspoon pepper**
1½ **pounds boneless lamb, cut into**
    ¾-inch cubes
  ½ **cup chopped onion**
  2 **cloves garlic, minced**
  3 **tablespoons olive oil *or* cooking oil**
  2 **cups beef broth**
  2 **medium potatoes, peeled and thinly**
    sliced (2 cups)
  2 **cups shelled peas *or* one 10-ounce**
    package frozen peas

In a plastic bag combine flour, salt, oregano, and pepper. Add meat and shake to coat; set aside. In a Dutch oven cook onion and garlic in hot oil till onion is tender; remove from pan. Brown meat, half at a time. Drain off fat. Return all meat and the onion mixture to pan; stir in beef broth and potatoes. Cover and simmer for 30 minutes. Add peas and cook 10 to 12 minutes or till meat and vegetables are tender. If desired, serve with grated Parmesan cheese. Makes 6 servings.

Curried Lamb Soup

  1 **medium onion, chopped**
  1 **medium apple, peeled and chopped**
  3 **to 4 teaspoons curry powder**
  ¼ **cup butter *or* margarine**
  3 **cups chicken broth**
1½ **cups diced cooked lamb**
  1 **cup cooked rice**
  ¼ **cup raisins**
  ¼ **teaspoon salt**
    Dash pepper
  ⅓ **cup dairy sour cream**
  ¼ **cup coarsely chopped peanuts**

In a large saucepan cook the onion, apple, and curry powder in the butter or margarine till the onion is tender. Stir in the broth, lamb, rice, raisins, salt, and pepper. Bring to boiling. Reduce heat. Cover and simmer 15 minutes. Gradually blend about 1 cup of the hot mixture into sour cream. Return all to saucepan and stir to combine thoroughly. Stir in peanuts. Makes 4 servings.

Creamy Chicken-Zucchini Soup

- 2 cups shredded zucchini
- ½ cup shredded carrot
- ½ cup chopped celery
- ½ cup water
- 2 tablespoons chopped onion
- 2 tablespoons snipped parsley
- 1 teaspoon seasoned salt
- 1 teaspoon instant chicken bouillon granules
- 2 tablespoons butter *or* margarine
- 2 tablespoons all-purpose flour
- ¼ teaspoon salt
- ⅛ teaspoon white pepper
- 1½ cups milk
- ½ cup light cream
- 1½ cups finely chopped cooked chicken

In a medium saucepan combine zucchini, carrot, celery, water, onion, parsley, seasoned salt, and bouillon granules. Cook about 5 minutes or till zucchini is tender. Place *half* of the *undrained* zucchini mixture in blender or food processor; cover and blend till smooth. Set aside. Repeat with remaining zucchini.

In a saucepan melt butter or margarine; stir in flour, salt, and pepper. Stir in milk and light cream. Cook and stir till thickened and bubbly. Stir in chicken and zucchini mixture. Cook and stir 5 minutes more or till heated through. Serves 4.

Serve this rich, colorful soup with fresh citrus salad & crusty onion rolls.

Savory Chicken Soup

- ¼ cup chopped onion
- ¼ cup sliced celery
- 1 clove garlic, minced
- 3 tablespoons butter *or* margarine
- 3 tablespoons all-purpose flour
- ½ teaspoon salt
- ¼ teaspoon dried marjoram, crushed
- ¼ teaspoon dried thyme, crushed
- 2½ cups milk
- 1 14½-ounce can chicken broth
- 1½ cups cubed cooked chicken
- 1 12-ounce can whole kernel corn with sweet peppers
- 1 cup cooked rice

In a saucepan cook onion, celery, and garlic in butter or margarine till vegetables are tender. Stir flour, salt, marjoram, and thyme into vegetable mixture, blending well. Stir in milk and broth. Cook and stir till slightly thickened and bubbly. Cook 1 to 2 minutes more. Stir in chicken, *undrained* corn, and rice. Continue cooking 5 to 10 minutes more or till heated through. Makes 4 to 6 servings.

Chicken-Parsnip Soup

- 1 cup cubed parsnips
- 1 cup cubed potatoes
- ½ cup chopped onion
- 3 tablespoons butter *or* margarine
- 2 tablespoons all-purpose flour
- ¼ teaspoon ground nutmeg
- 3½ cups milk
- 2 cups cubed cooked chicken
- 1 cup thinly sliced celery

In a 3-quart saucepan cook parsnips, potatoes, and onion in boiling salted water about 10 minutes or till tender. Drain, reserving ½ *cup* liquid. Place drained vegetables and reserved liquid in blender container or food processor bowl; cover and blend till chunky. Set aside.

In same saucepan melt butter or margarine; stir in flour, nutmeg, ½ teaspoon *salt,* and dash *pepper.* Add the milk; cook and stir till thickened and bubbly. Stir in the parsnip mixture, chicken, and celery. Heat through. Makes 6 servings.

Brunswick Stew

1 2½- to 3-pound broiler-fryer chicken, cut up
4 cups water
1 teaspoon salt
½ teaspoon celery salt
1 bay leaf
1 16-ounce can stewed tomatoes
1 10-ounce package frozen whole kernel corn
1 10-ounce package frozen lima beans
½ cup chopped onion
¼ cup chopped green pepper
1 tablespoon Worcestershire sauce
1 teaspoon sugar
¼ teaspoon ground red pepper
⅛ teaspoon ground ginger
⅛ teaspoon ground cumin
½ cup cold water
¼ cup all-purpose flour

Place chicken in a 5-quart Dutch oven. Add water, salt, celery salt, and bay leaf. Bring to boiling. Reduce heat; cover and simmer about 1 hour or till chicken is tender. Remove chicken from broth. Reserve *3 cups* of the broth; reserve remainder for another use. When chicken is cool enough to handle, remove skin and bones from chicken; discard skin and bones. Cut up chicken and set aside. Meanwhile, in Dutch oven combine reserved broth, *undrained* stewed tomatoes, the corn, lima beans, onion, green pepper, Worcestershire sauce, sugar, ground red pepper, ginger, and cumin. Bring to boiling; reduce heat. Cover and simmer 20 minutes. Combine water and flour; stir till smooth. Stir into stew along with chicken. Cook and stir till thickened and bubbly. Cook and stir 1 to 2 minutes more. Remove bay leaf. Serves 6.

Turkey and Vegetable Soup

2 14½-ounce cans chicken broth
1 16-ounce can stewed tomatoes
1½ cups vegetable juice cocktail
1 cup sliced carrots
1 9-ounce package frozen cut green beans
½ cup chopped onion
3 tablespoons onion-mushroom soup mix
1 tablespoon Worcestershire sauce
1 teaspoon instant beef bouillon granules
¼ teaspoon garlic powder
¼ teaspoon dried oregano, crushed
¼ teaspoon dried basil, crushed
2 cups cubed cooked turkey
1 cup medium noodles

In a stockpot or Dutch oven combine chicken broth, *undrained* stewed tomatoes, vegetable juice cocktail, carrots, green beans, onion, dry soup mix, Worcestershire, bouillon granules, garlic powder, oregano, basil, 1 cup *water,* and ⅛ teaspoon *pepper.* Bring to boiling; reduce heat. Cover and simmer 30 minutes, stirring occasionally. Add turkey and noodles. Bring to boiling. Cover; simmer 10 minutes more. Makes 6 servings.

Turkey-Asparagus Soup

¼ cup chopped celery
2 tablespoons chopped onion
2 tablespoons butter *or* margarine
3 cups milk
1 11-ounce can condensed cheddar cheese soup
1 teaspoon dry mustard
½ teaspoon Worcestershire sauce
¼ teaspoon salt
¼ cup packaged instant mashed potato flakes *or* buds
2 cups diced cooked turkey
1 10-ounce package frozen cut asparagus

In a medium saucepan cook celery and onion in butter or margarine till tender. Stir in milk, soup, mustard, Worcestershire sauce, and salt. Gradually stir in potato flakes or buds. Cook and stir till slightly thickened. Stir in turkey and asparagus. Cook 6 minutes more or till asparagus is tender. Makes 6 servings.

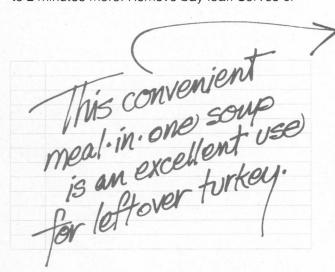

This convenient meal-in-one soup is an excellent use for leftover turkey.

Broccoli-Chicken Soup

2 6¾-ounce cans chunk-style chicken
3 tablespoons butter *or* margarine
¼ cup chopped onion
¼ cup all-purpose flour
1 teaspoon dry mustard
¼ teaspoon salt
¼ teaspoon dried thyme, crushed
⅛ teaspoon pepper
1¾ cups milk
1 14½-ounce can chicken broth
½ of a 20-ounce package (2 cups) frozen
   mixed broccoli, cauliflower, and
   carrots

Drain chicken, reserving liquid. Chop chicken, set aside. In a 3-quart saucepan melt butter or margarine; add onion and cook till tender but not browned. Stir in flour, dry mustard, salt, thyme, and pepper. Stir in milk and chicken broth all at once. Cook and stir over medium heat till slightly thickened and bubbly. Stir in vegetables, chicken, and chicken liquid. Cook and stir for 4 to 6 minutes more or till vegetables are tender and soup is heated through. Makes 6 servings.

Shrimp-Onion Bisque

3 tablespoons butter *or* margarine
1 medium onion, sliced and separated
   into rings
3 tablespoons all-purpose flour
¼ teaspoon pepper
1 14½-ounce can chicken broth
1 cup light cream
1 cup milk
1 7-ounce package frozen cooked shrimp,
   thawed and drained
½ cup shredded Swiss cheese
   Parmesan Croutons

In 3-quart saucepan melt butter or margarine; add onions and cook 7 to 8 minutes or till onion is tender. Stir in flour and pepper. Gradually stir in chicken broth, light cream, and milk. Cook and stir over medium heat till thickened and bubbly. Cook and stir 1 to 2 minutes more. Stir in shrimp and cheese. Continue cooking and stirring till cheese is melted. Place about ¼ cup Parmesan Croutons in each serving bowl; ladle soup over. Makes 4 servings.

Parmesan Croutons: Combine 1 cup fresh white *bread cubes* (1⅓ slices), 2 tablespoons melted *butter or margarine,* 2 teaspoons grated *Parmesan cheese,* ¼ teaspoon *garlic powder,* ¼ teaspoon *dry mustard,* and ¼ teaspoon *dried basil,* crushed. Toss to coat bread cubes. Place on baking sheet. Bake in 400° oven for 7 minutes or till browned, stirring once.

(Homemade Parmesan Croutons add a special flair to this elegant soup — but purchased croutons can also be used.)

Crab Soup

¼ cup butter *or* margarine
¼ cup all-purpose flour
4 cups milk
1 cup light cream
1 tablespoon Worcestershire sauce
2 teaspoons grated onion
¼ teaspoon ground mace
1¼ cups cooked crab meat, flaked and
   cartilage removed *or* one 6-ounce
   package frozen crab meat, thawed,
   drained, and cartilage removed
2 hard-cooked egg yolks, crumbled
¼ cup dry sherry

In saucepan melt butter or margarine; blend in flour till smooth. Add milk and cream, stirring constantly. Add Worcestershire, onion, mace, ½ teaspoon *salt,* and ¼ teaspoon *pepper;* cook and stir till bubbly. Cook and stir 1 to 2 minutes more. Add crab meat; heat through. To serve, place a *fourth* of the egg yolks and 1 *tablespoon* sherry in *each* bowl; ladle soup over. Makes 4 servings.

Curried Tuna Soup

1 medium apple, peeled and chopped
   (1 cup)
1 medium onion, chopped (½ cup)
2 teaspoons curry powder
¼ cup butter *or* margarine
4 cups chicken broth
¼ cup long grain rice
1 9¼-ounce can tuna, drained and flaked
½ teaspoon finely shredded lemon peel
½ cup dairy sour cream
2 tablespoons all-purpose flour

In a medium saucepan cook apple, onion, and curry powder in butter or margarine till onion is tender but not brown. Add chicken broth. Bring to boiling. Stir in *uncooked* rice; reduce heat. Cover and cook over low heat for 20 minutes or till rice is tender. Stir in tuna and lemon peel; heat through. Stir together sour cream and flour; gradually stir about 1 cup hot mixture into sour cream. Return to remaining hot mixture. Cook and stir till thickened and bubbly, but *do not boil.* Makes 4 servings.

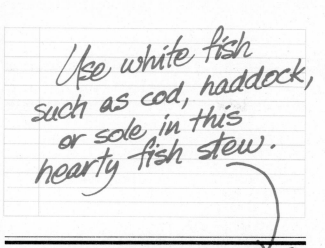

Use white fish such as cod, haddock, or sole in this hearty fish stew.

Monterey Fish Stew

1 pound fresh *or* frozen firm, white fish
1 small onion, diced (⅓ cup)
1 clove garlic, minced
2 tablespoons butter *or* margarine
1 cup water
⅓ cup dry vermouth
2 teaspoons instant chicken bouillon
    granules
¾ teaspoon salt
½ teaspoon dried marjoram, crushed
⅛ teaspoon pepper
1 bay leaf
2 potatoes, peeled and sliced (2 cups)
1 carrot, sliced (½ cup)
2 medium tomatoes, peeled and chopped
    (½ cup)
5 or 6 fresh mushrooms, quartered
2 tablespoons snipped parsley
¼ cup cold water
2 tablespoons cornstarch

Thaw fish, if frozen; cut fish into bite-size pieces. In a 3-quart saucepan cook onion and garlic in butter or margarine till tender but not brown. Stir in the 1 cup water, the vermouth, bouillon granules, salt, marjoram, pepper, and bay leaf. Add potatoes and carrot; bring to boiling. Reduce heat; cover and simmer about 20 minutes or till vegetables are just tender. Add fish, tomatoes, mushrooms, and parsley. Cover and simmer about 5 minutes or till fish flakes easily with a fork.

Remove fish; set aside. Combine the ¼ cup cold water and cornstarch; stir into saucepan. Cook and stir till thickened and bubbly. Cook and stir 1 to 2 minutes more. Return fish to saucepan; heat through. Makes 4 servings.

Salmon Chowder

½ cup chopped onion
½ cup chopped celery
3 tablespoons butter *or* margarine
3 tablespoons all-purpose flour
¼ teaspoon dried dillweed
¼ teaspoon garlic powder
⅛ teaspoon pepper
3½ cups milk
1 teaspoon instant chicken bouillon
    granules
1 cup shredded American cheese
    (4 ounces)
1 15½-ounce can pink salmon

In a large saucepan cook onion and celery in butter or margarine till tender but not brown. Stir in flour, dillweed, garlic powder, and pepper. Stir in milk and bouillon granules. Cook and stir till thickened and bubbly. Cook and stir 1 to 2 minutes more. Stir in cheese and heat till cheese melts. Drain salmon; remove skin and bones. Break salmon into chunks; add to chowder. Heat through. Makes 5 servings.

Potato Clam Soup

2 slices bacon, chopped
1 cup chopped onion
2 tablespoons all-purpose flour
1 teaspoon salt
¼ teaspoon dried savory, crushed
¼ teaspoon dried thyme, crushed
⅛ teaspoon pepper
2 6½-ounce cans minced clams
4 medium potatoes, peeled and cut into
    ½-inch cubes (4 cups)
2 cups milk
2 tablespoons snipped parsley

In saucepan cook bacon till almost crisp. Add onion and cook till tender. Stir in flour, salt, savory, thyme, and pepper. Drain clams, reserving liquid. Set clams aside. Stir reserved clam liquid and 1 cup *water* into saucepan. Add potatoes. Bring to boiling; reduce heat. Cover and simmer 15 to 20 minutes, stirring occasionally. Stir in clams, milk, and parsley. Heat through. Makes 6 servings.

Cubed cheese tops this hearty herb-flavored soup, chock-full of fresh garden vegetables.

Vegetable-Cheese Soup

  1 cup dry navy beans
  8 cups cold water
  8 cups hot water
  1 15-ounce can tomato sauce
  2 medium carrots, chopped (1 cup)
  1 medium onion, chopped (½ cup)
  2 cloves garlic, minced
  2 tablespoons instant beef bouillon
    granules
  2 cups coarsely chopped cabbage
  1 medium zucchini, sliced
  1 teaspoon dried basil, crushed
  ¾ teaspoon dried oregano, crushed
  ½ teaspoon dried thyme, crushed
  ½ cup elbow macaroni
  2 cups cubed Monterey Jack *or* American
    cheese (8 ounces)

In a large saucepan combine beans and cold water. Bring to boiling; reduce heat and simmer 2 minutes. Remove from heat. Cover; let stand 1 hour. (Or, soak beans in the water overnight in a covered pan.) Drain and rinse soaked beans; add the 8 cups hot water. Bring to boiling. Reduce heat. Cover and simmer 2 hours. Add tomato sauce, carrots, onion, garlic, and bouillon granules. Cover and simmer for 30 minutes.

Add cabbage, zucchini, basil, oregano, and thyme to soup. Bring to boiling; stir in macaroni. Reduce heat; simmer, uncovered, for 10 to 15 minutes or just till macaroni is tender. Ladle soup into individual serving bowls. Sprinkle each serving with cubes of Monterey Jack or American cheese. Makes 6 servings.

Beer-Cheese Soup

  ½ cup shredded carrot
  ¼ cup finely chopped onion
  ¼ cup butter *or* margarine
  3 tablespoons all-purpose flour
  1 teaspoon instant chicken bouillon
    granules
  ½ teaspoon salt
  ¼ teaspoon dry mustard
  ⅛ teaspoon ground ginger
  ⅛ teaspoon pepper
  3 cups milk
  1½ cups shredded cheddar cheese
    (6 ounces)
  ½ cup beer

In a medium saucepan cook shredded carrot and chopped onion in butter or margarine till tender. Stir in flour, instant chicken bouillon granules, salt, dry mustard, ground ginger, and pepper. Stir in milk all at once, mixing till smooth. Cook and stir over medium heat till thickened and bubbly. Cook and stir 1 minute more. Reduce heat; add cheddar cheese and beer and continue cooking and stirring till cheese is melted and soup is heated through. Makes 4 servings.

Cooking with Cheese

When using cheese in soups and stews, use low heat and be careful not to overcook. High temperatures and prolonged cooking will toughen the cheese. As a result, it will be stringy and curdled. Remember, when cheese is melted, it is cooked. Do not continue to heat it. Cheese that is shredded or cut into small pieces will melt the best.

One Dish Meals

Salads & Sandwiches

Truly full meals in themselves, these satisfying salads and sandwiches abound with freshness and a variety of flavors, colors, and textures. Plentiful with meat, poultry, seafood and cheese, crisp salad greens, and garden vegetables, all offer meals that are a change of pace. Many recipes here lend themselves perfectly to lighter meals such as brunch, luncheon, or supper. Keep them in mind, too, for the casual fare of a sultry summer day.

Create·a·Salad

Triple-Cheese Garden Salad

⅔ cup dairy sour cream
⅓ cup mayonnaise
¼ cup crumbled blue cheese
2 tablespoons vinegar
½ teaspoon garlic salt
½ teaspoon celery seed
3 cups torn salad greens
1 9- *or* 10-ounce package frozen cut
   vegetable, thawed and drained
1½ cups thinly sliced cucumber
4 ounces cheese, cut into julienne strips
1 cup diced cooked meat *or* one 6½-ounce
   can tuna, drained and flaked
¾ cup cubed sharp cheddar cheese
½ cup sliced pitted ripe olives
1 large tomato, cut into 8 wedges

For dressing, in a small bowl combine sour cream, mayonnaise, crumbled blue cheese, vinegar, garlic salt, celery seed, and ⅛ teaspoon *pepper;* mix well and chill while preparing salad.

In a large salad bowl combine desired greens, desired vegetable, sliced cucumber, desired cheese, desired meat or the tuna, cheddar cheese, olives, and tomato wedges. Pour dressing over and toss to coat. Makes 6 servings.

*Greens
Options*
spinach
Boston lettuce)
iceberg lettuce)
romaine)

*Cheese
Options*
Swiss
Edam
Gouda
brick

Vegetable Options
asparagus
broccoli
Italian green beans

Meat Options
chicken
beef
ham

Create·a·Sandwich

Supper Sandwich Supreme

¼ cup mayonnaise
¼ cup dairy sour cream
1½ teaspoons minced dried onion
1 teaspoon prepared horseradish
1 teaspoon prepared mustard
Dash garlic powder
12 slices bread
Butter or margarine, softened
12 ounces thinly sliced cooked meat
1 cup shredded cheese (4 ounces)
1 medium cucumber *or* 1 medium green
pepper *or* 1 cup bean sprouts (see
Vegetable Options)
6 lettuce leaves

For dressing, in a small bowl combine mayonnaise, sour cream, dried onion, horseradish, mustard, and garlic powder; mix well and set aside. Spread bread slices with softened butter or margarine. Place desired meat and cheese options on *six* slices of bread. Top *each* with about 1½ tablespoons dressing. Then top with vegetable option, lettuce leaves, and remaining bread slices. Halve sandwiches to serve. Makes 6 servings.

Cheese Options
cheddar
mozzarella
Swiss

Bread Options
whole wheat
rye
pumpernickel

Meat Options
roast beef
chicken
ham

Vegetable Options
cucumber, sliced
green pepper, cut into strips
bean sprouts

Chutneyed Chicken-Cabbage Salad

1 large chicken breast, split, skinned, and boned
1 tablespoon soy sauce
1 teaspoon grated gingerroot *or* ½ teaspoon ground ginger
1 tablespoon cooking oil
⅓ cup mayonnaise *or* salad dressing
⅓ cup chutney, chopped
1 tablespoon soy sauce
½ teaspoon curry powder
2 cups shredded Chinese cabbage
2 cups torn fresh spinach
1 8-ounce can pineapple chunks, drained
½ cup thinly sliced carrots
¼ cup chopped peanuts

Cut chicken into 1½x½-inch pieces. In a small bowl combine chicken, 1 tablespoon soy sauce, and the ginger, stirring to coat. Cover and marinate 2 hours in refrigerator. In a large skillet or wok stir-fry chicken in hot oil till done. Drain, cover, and chill. In a bowl stir together mayonnaise or salad dressing, chutney, 1 tablespoon soy sauce, and the curry powder. Toss with chicken, cabbage, spinach, drained pineapple, carrots, and peanuts. Serve in cabbage-lined bowl, if desired. Makes 4 to 6 servings.

Confetti Hamburger Salad

1 0.7-ounce envelope cheese-garlic salad dressing mix
⅓ cup water
2 tablespoons white wine vinegar
1 16-ounce can red kidney beans, drained
1 8-ounce can whole kernel corn, drained
2 tablespoons sliced green onion
6 cups torn mixed salad greens
½ cup coarsely shredded carrot
1 pound ground beef
2 tablespoons snipped parsley
1 tablespoon white wine vinegar
3 hard-cooked eggs, cut into wedges

Combine *half* the salad dressing mix (4 teaspoons), the water, and the 2 tablespoons wine vinegar. Add beans, corn, and green onion, stirring to coat. Cover and chill at least 2 hours, stirring several times. Line a large salad bowl with some

of the salad greens. Toss together remaining greens and carrot. Add to salad bowl; cover and chill. At serving time, brown ground beef; drain meat, reserving 2 tablespoons drippings. Stir parsley, the 1 tablespoon wine vinegar, and the remaining salad dressing mix into meat and reserved drippings. Heat through. Add bean mixture and the ground beef to salad greens. Toss gently to coat. Garnish salad with egg wedges. Serve at once. Makes 6 servings.

Wonton Chicken Salad

¼ cup cooking oil
¼ cup vinegar
2 tablespoons sugar
1 tablespoon sesame oil *or* cooking oil
10 wonton skins (3-inch squares)
Cooking oil
6 cups torn spinach
2 cups cubed cooked chicken
1 11-ounce can mandarin orange sections, drained
1 medium green *or* sweet red pepper, cut into ½-inch squares
4 green onions, bias sliced into 1-inch pieces

For dressing, in a screw-top jar combine the ¼ cup oil, the vinegar, sugar, sesame or cooking oil, 1 teaspoon *salt,* and ¼ teaspoon *pepper.* Cover; shake well. Chill. Cut wonton skins into ¼-inch-wide strips; fry, a few at a time, in shallow hot oil about ½ to 1 minute or till crisp and golden, stirring occasionally. Drain on paper toweling. Line a salad bowl with torn spinach. Over the spinach arrange chicken, drained mandarin oranges, green or red pepper, green onions, and fried wonton strips. Shake dressing; pour some over salad and toss to coat. Pass remaining dressing. Makes 6 servings.

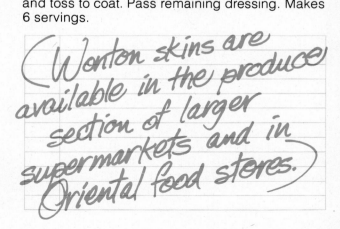
Wonton skins are available in the produce section of larger supermarkets and in Oriental food stores.

Layered Tuna Toss

2 cups broccoli flowerets
½ cup sliced carrots
6 cups torn spinach
1 cup sliced celery
1 9¼-ounce can tuna, drained and broken into large pieces
2 small tomatoes, cut into 6 wedges each
1 cup shredded Swiss cheese (4 ounces)
¾ cup dairy sour cream
⅓ cup plain yogurt
½ cup grated drained cucumber
½ teaspoon garlic salt

In covered saucepan cook broccoli and carrots in 1 inch of boiling salted water for 3 to 5 minutes or just till crisp-tender. Drain well; set aside. In large salad bowl layer *half* of the spinach, the broccoli and carrots, celery, tuna, tomatoes, the remaining spinach, and the cheese. For dressing, combine sour cream, yogurt, cucumber, and garlic salt. Spoon dressing over salad, spreading to edges; cover. Refrigerate 2 to 24 hours. Toss before serving. Serves 6.

Peanut-Chicken Salad

pictured on page 5

½ cup plain yogurt
⅓ cup peanut butter
¼ cup milk
3 tablespoons white wine vinegar
1 tablespoon sugar
1 tablespoon salad oil
½ teaspoon soy sauce
¼ teaspoon garlic powder
    Dash ground red pepper
6 cups torn mixed salad greens
2 cups diced cooked chicken
1 tart apple, cored and cut into thin wedges
1 cup shredded red cabbage
½ cup peanuts
¼ cup raisins
1 tablespoon thinly sliced green onion

For dressing, stir together yogurt, peanut butter, milk, vinegar, sugar, oil, soy, garlic powder, and red pepper. In a large salad bowl arrange greens, chicken, apple, cabbage, peanuts, raisins, and green onion. Add dressing; toss. Serves 6.

Pizza Salad

1 8-ounce can tomato sauce
½ cup salad oil
¼ cup white wine vinegar
1 teaspoon sugar
1 teaspoon dried oregano, crushed
¼ teaspoon garlic powder
1 medium head lettuce, torn (6 cups)
8 ounces sliced salami, cut into 1½-inch strips
1 cup shredded mozzarella cheese
1 cup shredded cheddar cheese
2 medium tomatoes, chopped
1 green pepper, chopped
½ cup pitted ripe olives, halved
1 tablespoon snipped chives

In a screw-top jar combine tomato sauce, oil, vinegar, sugar, oregano, garlic powder, 1 teaspoon *salt,* and ⅛ teaspoon *pepper;* cover and shake. Chill. Combine lettuce, salami, cheeses, tomatoes, green pepper, olives, and chives. Shake dressing; pour some over salad. Toss to coat. Pass remaining dressing. Makes 6 servings.

Salade Russe

3 large potatoes, cooked, peeled, and diced (3 cups)
2 cups cubed cooked chicken
1 cup frozen peas, thawed and drained
½ cup chopped green pepper
⅓ cup chopped dill pickle
3 tablespoons sliced green onion
1 cup mayonnaise *or* salad dressing
½ cup dairy sour cream
2 tablespoons lemon juice
    Lettuce leaves

In a large bowl combine potatoes, chicken, peas, green pepper, dill pickle, and green onion; toss gently to combine. Combine mayonnaise, sour cream, lemon juice, ¼ teaspoon *salt,* and dash *pepper;* mix well. Add mayonnaise mixture to chicken mixture, tossing gently till well combined. Chill 2 to 3 hours. To serve, mound salad on a lettuce-lined serving platter. If desired, sprinkle with dillweed and garnish with pimiento strips and 1 hard-cooked egg, cut into wedges. Serves 6.

Fruited Chicken Salad

4 cups diced cooked chicken
1 15-ounce can pineapple chunks, drained
1 11-ounce can mandarin orange sections,
   drained
1 cup chopped celery
½ cup sliced pitted ripe olives
½ cup chopped green pepper
2 tablespoons grated onion
1 cup mayonnaise *or* salad dressing
1 tablespoon prepared mustard
1 5-ounce can chow mein noodles
   Lettuce leaves

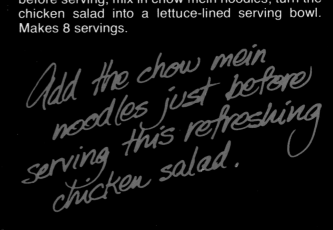

In a large bowl combine cooked chicken, pineapple chunks, oranges, celery, olives, green pepper, and onion. Stir together mayonnaise or salad dressing and mustard; toss gently with chicken mixture. Cover and chill several hours. Just before serving, mix in chow mein noodles; turn the chicken salad into a lettuce-lined serving bowl. Makes 8 servings.

Add the chow mein noodles just before serving this refreshing chicken salad.

Reuben Salad

1 cup dairy sour cream
¼ cup chili sauce
2 tablespoons sliced green onion
1 tablespoon sugar
1 16-ounce can sauerkraut, rinsed and drained
¼ cup chopped dill pickle
¼ cup snipped parsley
6 cups torn lettuce
½ pound thinly sliced cooked corned beef, cut into julienne strips
1½ cups shredded Swiss cheese (6 ounces)
3 slices rye bread
1 tablespoon butter or margarine

For dressing, in a small bowl combine sour cream, chili sauce, green onion, sugar, and ¼ teaspoon *salt*. Set aside. Combine the sauerkraut, dill pickle, and parsley; set aside.

In a large salad bowl layer *3 cups* of the lettuce, the sauerkraut mixture, corned beef, Swiss cheese, and the remaining lettuce. Spread dressing evenly over top of salad. Cover and chill for 2 hours. For croutons, cut rye bread into ½-inch cubes. Melt butter or margarine in a 10-inch skillet. Add bread cubes. Cook and stir over medium-high heat about 6 minutes or till toasted. Set aside. To serve, add croutons to salad; toss. Serves 6.

Shrimp-Snap Pea Salad

¼ cup salad oil
2 tablespoons Dijon-style mustard
2 tablespoons lemon juice
½ teaspoon celery seed
2 slices onion
2 bay leaves
4 whole peppercorns
1 pound fresh or frozen shrimp in shells
1½ cups sugar snap peas (6 ounces)
6 cups torn mixed salad greens
Leaf lettuce
Alfalfa sprouts

In a screw-top jar combine salad oil, mustard, lemon juice, celery seed, and dash *pepper*. Cover and shake; chill. In a medium saucepan combine onion, bay leaves, peppercorns, and 3 cups *water;* bring to boiling. Reduce heat; simmer 5 minutes. Add shrimp; return to boiling. Reduce heat and simmer, covered, 1 to 3 minutes or till shrimp turn pink. Drain; peel and clean. Cover and chill. Remove strings from peas. Cook peas till crisp-tender, if desired. Chill.

At serving time, place greens in a large bowl; add chilled shrimp and peas. Shake dressing; pour over salad. Toss to coat. Serve on individual lettuce-lined plates; garnish with alfalfa sprouts. Makes 4 servings.

Curried Turkey Waldorf Salad

¾ cup dairy sour cream
2 tablespoons milk
1 teaspoon lemon juice
½ teaspoon curry powder
⅛ teaspoon salt
2 cups diced cooked turkey
1 large apple, cored and diced
½ cup chopped celery
½ cup halved and seeded red grapes
½ cup chopped walnuts

For dressing, in a small bowl combine sour cream, milk, lemon juice, curry powder, and salt; mix well. In a medium bowl combine turkey, apple, celery, grapes, and walnuts. Spoon dressing over turkey mixture and toss to coat. Cover and chill for at least 1 hour. Serve on lettuce-lined salad plates, if desired. Makes 4 servings.

Preparing Salad Greens

To prepare salad greens for use, remove and discard any wilted outer leaves. For thorough rinsing, remove core from head lettuce; separate leafy lettuce. Rinse the greens in cold water. Drain. Place leafy greens in a clean kitchen towel or paper toweling, and pat or toss gently to remove clinging water. Tear greens into bite-size pieces.

Pineapple and Ham Salad

Cucumber Dressing
2 small fresh pineapples, chilled
3 cups torn lettuce
2 cups diced fully cooked ham
1 avocado, halved, seeded, peeled, and
   sliced
Lemon juice

Prepare Cucumber Dressing; set aside. Halve pineapples lengthwise. Using a sharp knife cut out pineapple meat, leaving shells intact. Reserve shells. Cut out hard core; cut pineapple into large chunks. Combine lettuce, ham, and *3 cups* of the pineapple chunks (refrigerate remaining pineapple for another use); toss. Spoon the ham mixture into pineapple shells. Brush avocado slices with lemon juice. Garnish each salad with avocado slices. Pass dressing. Makes 4 servings.

Cucumber Dressing: In small bowl combine ¼ cup *mayonnaise,* ¼ cup *dairy sour cream,* 2 tablespoons chopped *cucumber,* ¼ teaspoon *garlic salt,* and dash bottled *hot pepper sauce.*

Hot Chicken Salad

1 9-ounce package frozen Italian green
   beans, cooked and drained
1½ cups cubed cooked chicken
1½ cups shredded cheddar cheese
1 cup sliced celery
3 slices bacon, crisp cooked, drained,
   and crumbled
2 tablespoons chopped pimiento
1 8-ounce container sour cream dip with
   French onion
½ cup mayonnaise *or* salad dressing
¼ cup milk
1 tablespoon all-purpose flour
   Dash garlic powder
½ cup cornflakes

In bowl combine beans, chicken, cheese, celery, bacon, and pimiento. Combine sour cream dip, mayonnaise or salad dressing, milk, flour, garlic powder, and dash *pepper;* mix well. Pour sour cream mixture over chicken mixture; toss to coat. Turn into an 8x8x2-inch baking dish. Sprinkle with cornflakes. Bake in a 325° oven for 35 to 40 minutes or till bubbly. Makes 6 servings.

Cheesy Sour Cream Potato Salad

6 large green peppers
5 medium potatoes (1¾ pounds)
3 hard-cooked eggs
10 ounces cheddar cheese, cut into ⅜-inch
   cubes (2½ cups)
½ cup sliced celery
¼ cup sliced green onion

1 cup dairy sour cream
½ cup mayonnaise *or* salad dressing
⅓ cup milk
2 tablespoons lemon juice
1 tablespoon sugar
2 teaspoons prepared mustard
1 teaspoon celery seed
½ teaspoon salt
¼ teaspoon pepper
   Paprika

Remove tops from green peppers. Cut peppers in half lengthwise and remove seeds. Cook peppers in boiling salted water for 3 to 5 minutes; invert to drain. Chill.

Cook potatoes in boiling salted water about 20 minutes or till tender. Peel and slice the potatoes. Slice *1* of the hard-cooked eggs; set aside to use as garnish. Chop the remaining *2* hard-cooked eggs. In a large bowl combine the sliced potatoes, chopped egg, cheese cubes, celery slices, and green onion; toss gently to mix.

In a bowl combine dairy sour cream, mayonnaise or salad dressing, milk, lemon juice, sugar, prepared mustard, celery seed, salt, and pepper; stir to blend. Add sour cream mixture to the potato mixture and toss gently to coat. Chill 3 to 4 hours or till mixture is thoroughly chilled. To serve, spoon the potato salad into the chilled green pepper halves. Garnish pepper cups with hard-cooked egg slices and sprinkle with paprika. Serves 6.

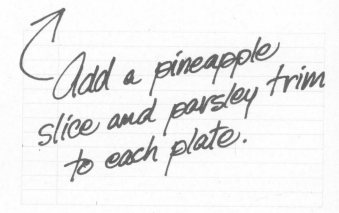
Add a pineapple slice and parsley trim to each plate.

Chef's Beef Sandwich

2 cups frozen loose-pack mixed broccoli, mushrooms, and red and green pepper (6 ounces)
1 medium onion, thinly sliced
1 tablespoon butter *or* margarine
6 club rolls, split
1 cup dairy sour cream
1 tablespoon horseradish mustard
12 thin slices cooked roast beef (about 8 ounces)
6 ounces sliced Monterey Jack *or* mozzarella cheese

In saucepan cook vegetables in boiling *unsalted* water for 6 to 8 minutes or till just tender. Drain and set aside. In same saucepan cook onion in butter or margarine till tender but not brown; set aside. Place rolls, cut side up, on baking sheet or shallow baking pan. Combine sour cream and horseradish mustard. Spread each roll half with about ½ *tablespoon* of the sour cream mixture; top with cooked onions. Spread remaining sour cream mixture over the beef slices. Spoon cooked mixed vegetables down center of each beef slice; roll up and place atop onions on roll halves. Cut cheese slices to fit and place atop beef rolls. Cover sandwiches loosely with foil. Bake in a 350° oven for 12 to 15 minutes or till sandwiches are heated through. Makes 6 servings.

Ham-Slaw Sandwiches

2 6¾-ounce cans chunk-style ham, flaked
1½ cups finely shredded cabbage
½ cup shredded carrot
⅓ cup mayonnaise *or* salad dressing
¼ cup chopped celery
2 tablespoons chili sauce
8 hard rolls
Butter *or* margarine, softened
Leaf lettuce
4 ounces cheddar cheese, cut into 8 cubes
8 cherry tomatoes
2 medium dill pickles, cut into fourths

In mixing bowl combine ham, shredded cabbage, shredded carrot, mayonnaise or salad dressing, chopped celery, and chili sauce. Cover and chill mixture.

Cut a thin slice from the top of each hard roll; scoop out centers, leaving a ½-inch rim on all sides. (Save the bread removed for use as bread crumbs in other recipes.) Spread the inside of each bread "shell" with butter or margarine and line with leaf lettuce. Fill each roll with about ⅓ *cup* of the ham-cabbage mixture.

Make kabobs to garnish each sandwich by spearing a cheese cube, cherry tomato, and pickle chunk on each of 8 short wooden skewers or picks. Insert one kabob into ham filling on each roll. Makes 8 sandwiches.

75

Spinach-Stuffed Ham Rolls

¼ cup butter *or* margarine, softened
2 teaspoons prepared horseradish
2 teaspoons prepared mustard
6 frankfurter buns, split
1 10-ounce package frozen chopped spinach
2 tablespoons chopped onion
¼ cup dairy sour cream
¼ cup chopped dill pickle
1 tablespoon steak sauce
6 slices boiled ham
6 slices Swiss cheese (6 ounces)

In a bowl combine the butter or margarine, horseradish, and mustard; stir to blend. Spread butter mixture on cut sides of frankfurter buns; set the buns aside.

In a saucepan cook spinach with the onion according to package directions; drain well, pressing out excess water from spinach. In saucepan combine the well-drained spinach, sour cream, dill pickle, and steak sauce; heat through. Place a ham slice on top of each cheese slice. Divide warm spinach mixture among the ham slices, spreading to edges. Roll cheese and ham up jelly-roll style. Place seam side down in buttered buns. Place buns in a 13x9x2-inch baking pan. Bake, covered, in a 400° oven for 12 to 15 minutes or till heated through. Makes 6 servings.

Avocado-Shrimp Rolls

  3 cups water
10 ounces fresh *or* frozen peeled and
       deveined shrimp
 ¼ cup salad oil
  2 tablespoons lemon juice
 ½ teaspoon salt
 ½ teaspoon sugar
       Dash pepper
       Dash paprika
 ½ cup crumbled blue cheese (2 ounces)

  1 medium avocado, halved, seeded,
       peeled, and cut up
 ¼ small onion
  1 tablespoon lemon juice
  1 small clove garlic, minced
 ¼ teaspoon salt
 ⅛ teaspoon pepper
  4 kaiser rolls, split lengthwise and toasted

Bring the 3 cups water to boiling. Add fresh or frozen shrimp. Return to boiling; reduce heat. Cover and simmer for 1 to 3 minutes or till shrimp turn pink. Drain. Cover and chill.

For marinade, in a screw-top jar combine oil, the 2 tablespoons lemon juice, the ½ teaspoon salt, the sugar, dash pepper, and paprika. Cover and shake well. Combine chilled shrimp and blue cheese. Pour marinade over; toss lightly to coat. Cover and chill several hours or overnight.

In blender container or food processor bowl combine avocado, onion, the 1 tablespoon lemon juice, garlic, the ¼ teaspoon salt, and ⅛ teaspoon pepper; cover and process till mixture is smooth. Spread avocado mixture on bottom halves of toasted kaiser rolls. Drain shrimp and blue cheese mixture. Spoon shrimp and cheese over avocado mixture. Add the toasted tops of kaiser rolls. Makes 4 servings.

Accompany these sandwiches with crisp corn chips & fresh fruit such as melon wedges & fresh berries.

Bean and Egg Sandwiches

  1 15½-ounce can red kidney beans,
       drained
 ⅓ cup chopped celery
  3 tablespoons sweet pickle relish
  2 tablespoons finely chopped onion
 ¼ cup mayonnaise *or* salad dressing
 ¼ teaspoon salt
 ¼ teaspoon dry mustard
  6 hamburger buns, split
  6 hard-cooked eggs, sliced
  3 slices American cheese, halved
       diagonally (3 ounces)

Combine kidney beans, celery, pickle relish, and onion. Stir together mayonnaise, salt, dry mustard, and dash *pepper*. Add to bean mixture; mix well. Spoon about ¼ *cup* bean mixture on bottom half of each bun; top with egg slices, then with one cheese triangle. Replace top halves of buns. Place on baking sheet; cover with foil. Bake in a 350° oven for 20 minutes or till sandwiches are heated through. Makes 6 servings.

Mexican Hero Sandwiches

 ½ cup dairy sour cream
  3 tablespoons chopped canned green chili
       peppers
  2 tablespoons chili sauce
 ¼ teaspoon garlic salt
  1 small avocado, halved, seeded, peeled,
       and finely chopped
  2 tablespoons finely chopped onion
  4 6- to 7-inch individual French rolls
  8 ounces thinly sliced rare roast beef
  1 large tomato, sliced
  4 lettuce leaves

In a bowl combine sour cream, chili peppers, chili sauce, and garlic salt. Stir in avocado and onion; set aside. Split French rolls in half lengthwise; hollow out center of top and bottom part leaving a ½-inch shell. (Save the bread removed for use as bread crumbs in other recipes.) Spoon about *half* the sour cream mixture into bottom halves of the French rolls. Top with the roast beef, then tomato slices, lettuce, and remaining sour cream mixture. Add top half of French roll. Makes 4 servings.

Chicken and Bean Sprout Pockets

1 small avocado, seeded and peeled
2 teaspoons lemon juice
1½ cups chopped cooked chicken
 (8 ounces)
1 cup fresh bean sprouts *or* alfalfa sprouts
1 cup shredded lettuce
1 small tomato, diced (⅓ cup)
⅓ cup green goddess salad dressing
2 large pita bread rounds, halved

Dice the avocado and toss with lemon juice till coated. In a bowl toss together the avocado, chicken, bean or alfalfa sprouts, lettuce, and tomato. Fold in the green goddess salad dressing. Spoon some of the salad mixture into each pita bread pocket. Makes 4 servings.

Curried Turkey-Filled Pitas

¼ cup light raisins
 Boiling water
¼ cup chopped onion
2 tablespoons butter *or* margarine
2 cups cubed cooked turkey *or* chicken
½ of a 10¾-ounce can (about ⅔ cup)
 condensed cream of chicken soup
½ cup cooked *or* canned peas
¼ cup dairy sour cream
2 tablespoons milk
1 to 2 teaspoons curry powder
3 pita bread rounds, halved

In small bowl cover raisins with boiling water. Let stand 5 minutes; drain and set aside.

In saucepan cook onion in butter or margarine till onion is tender but not brown. Remove from heat and stir in the raisins, turkey or chicken, condensed cream of chicken soup, peas, dairy sour cream, milk, and curry powder. Spoon some of filling into each pita bread pocket. Place the filled pitas on baking sheet. Bake in a 375° oven about 10 minutes or till hot. Makes 6 servings.

Meatball Pockets

77

1 medium cucumber, finely chopped
1 large tomato, finely chopped
1 small onion, coarsely chopped
¼ cup olive oil *or* cooking oil
3 tablespoons white wine vinegar
½ teaspoon dried oregano, crushed
¼ teaspoon salt
¼ teaspoon pepper

1 beaten egg
¾ cup soft bread crumbs (1 slice)
½ cup milk
2 tablespoons finely chopped onion
1 teaspoon salt
1 teaspoon ground allspice
¼ teaspoon pepper
¾ pound lean ground beef
½ pound ground pork
4 pita bread rounds, halved

In a bowl combine cucumber, tomato, small onion, oil, wine vinegar, oregano, ¼ teaspoon salt, and ¼ teaspoon pepper. Cover; marinate in refrigerator several hours or overnight.

In bowl combine egg, bread crumbs, milk, the 2 tablespoons onion, 1 teaspoon salt, allspice, and ¼ teaspoon pepper. Add beef and pork; mix well. Shape into 24 meatballs. Place in a 12x7½x2-inch baking dish. Bake in a 375° oven for 25 to 30 minutes. Drain on paper toweling.

To assemble sandwiches, place 3 meatballs in each pita bread half. Top with some of the undrained cucumber mixture. Makes 8 servings.

Pocket Bread Sandwiches

To make sandwiches interesting, use pita bread instead of the traditional bread slices or buns. Pita bread is a large, thin round of bread that splits apart to form a pocket, thus the name "pocket bread." A popular way to use pita bread is to cut the rounds in half crosswise, forming two pockets. Then, fill the "pockets" with a sandwich filling, such as any of the three suggested on this page.

Guacamole Submarine Sandwich

1 8-ounce loaf unsliced French *or* Vienna
  bread (12 to 14 inches long)
1 medium avocado, halved, seeded,
  peeled, and cut up
2 green onions, sliced
2 tablespoons dairy sour cream
1 tablespoon lemon juice
¼ teaspoon salt
½ cup bean sprouts
4 ounces sliced cheddar cheese
2 2½-ounce packages thinly sliced cooked
  turkey
8 thin tomato slices

Cut bread into 16 slices about ¾ inch thick,
cutting to but not through bottom crust. In blender
container or food processor bowl combine avocado, green onions, sour cream, lemon juice, and
salt; cover and process till smooth. Stir in bean
sprouts. Spread avocado mixture on cut sides of
alternate bread slices. Cut cheese and fold turkey
as needed to fit bread slices. Tuck cheese, turkey,
and tomatoes into slits spread with avocado mixture. Place on baking sheet. Bake in a 350° oven
for 15 minutes or till crisp and hot. Cut bread apart
into sandwiches. Makes 4 servings.

Fruited Chicken Wedges

1 package (8) refrigerated crescent rolls
2½ cups finely chopped cooked chicken
½ cup sliced pitted ripe olives
½ cup finely chopped celery
2 tablespoons finely chopped onion
¾ cup dairy sour cream
½ teaspoon finely shredded orange peel
¼ teaspoon salt
½ cup sliced almonds
1 medium avocado, halved, seeded, peeled, and cut into 12 slices
Lemon juice
1 11-ounce can mandarin orange sections, drained

Unroll crescent-roll dough; separate into triangles. On a 12-inch ungreased pizza pan evenly space the triangles in a spoke fashion, with the points toward the center, to form a circle. Press dough with fingers to seal seams. Bake in a 375° oven for 10 minutes.

Meanwhile, in small bowl combine chicken, olives, celery, and onion. In another small bowl combine sour cream, orange peel, and salt. Add to the chicken mixture; toss lightly to coat. Spread the chicken mixture on the prebaked crust. Sprinkle with almonds. Bake 8 to 10 minutes or till heated through. Dip avocado slices in a mixture of lemon juice and a little water. Arrange avocado slices and mandarin orange sections atop the chicken mixture. Cut into wedges to serve. Serve immediately. Makes 6 servings.

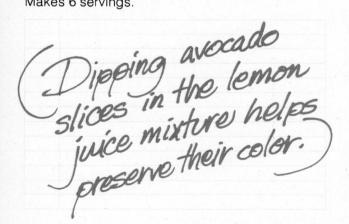

(Dipping avocado slices in the lemon juice mixture helps preserve their color.)

Ham and Cheese Vegetable-Wiches

79

1 3-ounce package cream cheese, softened
1 tablespoon milk
1 teaspoon prepared horseradish
1 teaspoon prepared mustard
⅛ teaspoon garlic powder
8 slices rye bread
4 lettuce leaves
8 slices boiled ham (8 ounces)
4 slices Swiss cheese (4 ounces)
16 thin tomato slices
16 thin cucumber slices

In a small bowl combine the softened cream cheese, milk, horseradish, mustard, and garlic powder. Stir till smooth. Spread *2 teaspoons* of the cream cheese mixture on each bread slice. Top *half* of the bread slices with lettuce, ham, cheese, tomato, and cucumber. Top with remaining bread slices. Slice in half and anchor with wooden picks. Makes 4 servings.

Open-Faced Reuben Sandwiches

2 brown-and-serve French rolls
⅓ cup Thousand Island salad dressing
1 tablespoon chopped onion
½ teaspoon caraway seed
2 2½-ounce packages thinly sliced cooked turkey
1 2½-ounce package thinly sliced cooked corned beef
1 8-ounce can sauerkraut, drained and patted dry
4 ounces sliced Swiss cheese

Bake French rolls according to package directions; cool. In small bowl combine salad dressing, onion, and caraway seed; mix well. Slice bread in half horizontally; spread each roll half with about *1 tablespoon* dressing mixture. Layer turkey, corned beef, sauerkraut, and Swiss cheese on each roll half. Drizzle remaining dressing mixture over all. Place sandwiches on baking sheet. Bake in a 350° oven for 10 to 12 minutes or till sandwiches are heated through and cheese is melted. Makes 4 servings.

Turkey Divan Sandwiches

1 10¾-ounce can condensed cream of
    chicken soup
1 cup shredded cheddar cheese
½ cup dairy sour cream
¼ cup dry white wine
¼ teaspoon dried marjoram, crushed
4 slices French bread, cut ½ inch thick
2 tablespoons butter, softened
4 slices boiled ham
4 slices cooked turkey (4 ounces)
1 10-ounce package frozen broccoli
    spears, cooked and drained

Combine first 5 ingredients; stir to blend.
Lightly toast bread; spread with butter. Place slices
into four individual 14-ounce casseroles. Top *each*
with 1 slice ham and 1 slice turkey. Divide broccoli
among the casseroles, placing atop turkey. Top
each casserole with about ½ *cup* of the soup mixture. Bake in a 400° oven for 15 to 20 minutes or till
heated through. Makes 4 servings.

Cheesy Chicken Salad Sandwiches

1 6¾-ounce can chunk-style chicken,
    drained and chopped
2 hard-cooked eggs, chopped
⅓ cup mayonnaise *or* salad dressing
⅓ cup chopped green pepper
¼ cup crumbled blue cheese
2 tablespoons sliced green onion
6 individual French rolls
    Butter *or* margarine, softened
6 slices Swiss cheese (6 ounces)

In a bowl combine chicken, hard-cooked
eggs, mayonnaise or salad dressing, green pepper, blue cheese, and green onion; mix well and
chill about 1½ hours. To serve, remove a thin slice
from top of each roll; hollow out center. (Save the
bread removed for use as bread crumbs in other
recipes.) Spread inside of each roll with butter or
margarine. Fold 1 slice Swiss cheese and place in
hollow of each roll. Spoon about ⅓ cup filling into
each roll. Replace tops. Makes 6 servings.

Salmon Bundles

1 3-ounce package cream cheese,
    softened
¼ cup cream-style cottage cheese
½ cup sliced celery
2 tablespoons finely chopped onion
1 teaspoon dried parsley flakes
½ teaspoon dried basil, crushed
½ teaspoon dried thyme, crushed
1 7¾-ounce can salmon, drained and
    flaked
1 package (8) refrigerated crescent rolls
1 tablespoon butter *or* margarine, melted
1 teaspoon sesame seed

In a bowl combine cream cheese and cottage cheese. Add celery, onion, parsley, basil, and
thyme; mix well. Fold in salmon. Separate crescent-roll dough into 4 rectangles; firmly press per-
forations to seal. Spoon about *one-fourth* of the
salmon mixture onto center of each rectangle. Pull
four corners of dough to top center of filling; pinch
to seal. Place on ungreased baking sheet. Brush
tops with melted butter; sprinkle with sesame seed.
Bake in a 350° oven for 20 to 25 minutes or till
golden. Makes 4 servings.

Deviled Ham-Chicken Sandwiches

1 4½-ounce can deviled ham
⅓ cup small curd cream-style cottage
    cheese
¼ cup mayonnaise *or* salad dressing
¼ cup chopped celery
2 tablespoons chopped dill pickle, drained
1 teaspoon prepared horseradish
1 teaspoon prepared mustard
10 slices whole wheat bread, toasted
5 ounces sliced cooked chicken *or* turkey
5 slices Monterey Jack cheese (5 ounces)
5 slices tomato (1 large)
5 lettuce leaves

In a small bowl combine deviled ham, cottage cheese, mayonnaise or salad dressing, celery, dill pickle, horseradish, and mustard; mix well.
On *half* of the toasted bread slices layer 2 tablespoons ham mixture, sliced chicken, Monterey
Jack cheese, 2 more tablespoons ham mixture,
tomato slices, and lettuce. Top each with another
toasted bread slice. Cut sandwiches in half to
serve. Makes 5 servings.

One Dish Meals

International Favorites

Moussaka, beef bourguignonne, enchiladas, paella—these and many other popular one-dish meals that originated in other lands are presented here. Many have become widely known in this country; others may be a bit more unfamiliar to most cooks. But all offer meals with a hint of extra excitement. Most of these hearty dishes require only the addition of a salad, a dessert, and a beverage to round out an out-of-the-ordinary meal.

Lasagna with Green Noodles

Italy

1¼ cups torn spinach
1 egg
1¼ cups all-purpose flour
1 pound ground beef
1 16-ounce can tomatoes, cut up
½ cup dry white wine
½ cup chopped onion
¼ cup chopped celery
¼ cup chopped carrot
2 tablespoons snipped parsley
½ teaspoon instant beef bouillon granules
⅛ teaspoon ground nutmeg
¼ cup butter *or* margarine
¼ cup all-purpose flour
⅛ teaspoon white pepper
⅛ teaspoon ground nutmeg
2 cups milk
1 cup grated Parmesan cheese

To make noodles, in small saucepan combine spinach and 2 tablespoons *water.* Cover and cook till spinach is very tender. Cool slightly; place spinach and liquid in blender container. Add egg and ½ teaspoon *salt.* Cover and blend till smooth. Transfer to a bowl. Add enough of the 1¼ cups flour to make a stiff dough. Knead on lightly floured surface 8 minutes. Cover and let rest 10 minutes. Divide dough in half. Roll each half to a rectangle 11x9 inches. Cut each half into three 11x3-inch strips. Add noodles to boiling salted water, stirring gently with a spoon. Bring to boiling and cook 1 minute. Carefully remove noodles; dip in cold water and lay each strip on paper toweling while preparing sauces.

To make meat sauce, in large skillet cook beef till browned; drain off excess fat. Add *undrained* tomatoes, the wine, onion, celery, carrot, parsley, bouillon granules, ⅛ teaspoon nutmeg, and ¼ cup *water.* Bring to boiling; reduce heat. Boil gently, uncovered, for 45 minutes or till desired consistency; stir occasionally.

To make white sauce, in saucepan melt butter or margarine. Stir in ¼ cup flour, white pepper, ⅛ teaspoon nutmeg, and ¼ teaspoon *salt.* Add the milk. Cook and stir till thickened and bubbly.

To assemble, arrange a single layer of the green noodles in the bottom of a greased 12x7½x2-inch baking dish. Spread with *half* of the meat sauce, *half* of the white sauce, and ½ *cup* of the Parmesan. Repeat layers with green noodles, meat sauce, white sauce, and cheese. Cover dish and bake in a 350° oven for 40 to 50 minutes. Makes 6 to 8 servings.

Pizza

Italy

2½ to 3 cups all-purpose flour
1 package active dry yeast
1 teaspoon salt
1 cup warm water (115° to 120°)
2 tablespoons cooking oil

1 pound mozzarella *or* provolone cheese, shredded (4 cups)
4 medium tomatoes, peeled and chopped (2 cups)
8 ounces diced fully cooked ham (1½ cups)
1 4-ounce can sliced mushrooms, drained
1 tablespoon olive oil
1 teaspoon dried oregano, crushed
1 teaspoon dried basil, crushed

In large mixer bowl combine *1¼ cups* of the flour, the yeast, and salt. Add warm water and the 2 tablespoons cooking oil. Beat at low speed of electric mixer for ½ minute, scraping sides of bowl. Beat 3 minutes at high speed. Stir in as much of the remaining flour as you can mix in with a spoon. Turn out onto a lightly floured surface. Knead in enough remaining flour to make a moderately stiff dough that is smooth and elastic (5 to 8 minutes total). Cover dough and let rest 10 minutes. Divide the dough in half.

On lightly floured surface roll each half of dough into a 13-inch circle. Transfer dough circles to two greased 12-inch pizza pans. Build up edges slightly. Bake in a 425° oven about 12 minutes or till the crusts are lightly browned.

Sprinkle *half* the mozzarella or provolone cheese over crusts. Divide chopped tomatoes, diced ham, and sliced mushrooms atop both pizzas. Drizzle the 1 tablespoon olive oil over the topping ingredients; sprinkle with crushed oregano and basil. Sprinkle remaining mozzarella or provolone cheese atop. Return to the 425° oven and bake for 10 to 15 minutes more or till topping is bubbly. Makes 8 servings (two 12-inch pizzas).

Green Bean Frittata

Italy

½ cup chopped onion
2 tablespoons cooking oil
1 8-ounce can French-style green beans
   or wax beans, drained (1 cup)
6 eggs
½ cup grated Parmesan cheese
¼ cup milk
2 tablespoons snipped parsley (optional)
⅛ teaspoon pepper

In 10-inch skillet with oven-proof handle cook onion in hot oil till tender but not brown. Spread the drained beans over onions in skillet. In mixing bowl beat together the eggs, Parmesan cheese, milk, parsley, and pepper. Pour over the vegetables in skillet. Cook over medium heat without stirring till set around outer edge. As eggs set, run a spatula around edge of skillet, lifting egg mixture to allow uncooked portion to flow underneath. Continue cooking and lifting edges till top of frittata is almost set (surface will be moist). Cooking time is 4 to 6 minutes. Place pan under broiler 5 inches from heat. Broil 1 to 2 minutes or till top is set. Cut into wedges to serve. Makes 4 servings.

Pea Soup

Holland

1 pound dry green split peas (2¼ cups)
6 cups water
2 pounds fresh pigs' feet
1 cup chopped onion
1 cup chopped celery
2 teaspoons salt
½ of a 12-ounce package fully cooked
   smoked sausage links, sliced
   Snipped parsley

Rinse peas. Place in Dutch oven. Add the water, pigs' feet, onion, celery, and salt. Bring to boiling. Reduce heat; cover and simmer for 1½ hours. Remove pigs' feet; cut off any meat and chop. Return meat to soup; discard bones. Add the sliced sausage. Heat through. Garnish with parsley. Serve with pumpernickel bread, if desired. Makes 6 to 8 servings.

Individual Pork Pies

Canada

2 cups all-purpose flour
1 teaspoon salt
⅔ cup shortening
6 to 7 tablespoons cold water

1 pound boneless pork, finely chopped
½ cup chopped onion
2 slices bacon, chopped
1 cup beef broth
1 clove garlic, minced
¼ teaspoon salt
⅛ teaspoon pepper
⅛ teaspoon ground nutmeg

¼ cup cold water
3 tablespoons all-purpose flour
   Milk

In medium mixing bowl stir together the flour and salt. Cut in the shortening till pieces are the size of small peas. Sprinkle 1 tablespoon of the first cold water over part of the mixture. Gently toss with a fork; push to side of bowl. Repeat till all is moistened. Form the dough into a ball. Divide the dough into 8 parts. On a floured surface roll out 4 of the parts into 7-inch circles. Fit the pastry rounds into four 4- or 6-inch tart pans; set aside.

Meanwhile, in skillet cook the pork, onion, and bacon till meat is browned. Add the beef broth, garlic, salt, pepper, and nutmeg. Cover and simmer about 30 minutes or till meat is tender. Combine the ¼ cup cold water and the 3 tablespoons flour. Stir into meat mixture; cook and stir till mixture is thickened and bubbly. Divide the hot mixture among the pastry-lined tart pans. Roll out the remaining 4 portions of dough into 7-inch rounds. Adjust the top crusts over filling. Fold extra pastry under bottom crusts. Seal and flute edges. Cut slits in top crusts for escape of steam. Brush pastry with a little milk. Bake in a 400° oven for 25 to 30 minutes. Makes 4 servings.

Pork and Sauerkraut Skillet

Germany

1 medium onion, sliced
2 tablespoons butter *or* margarine
1 16-ounce can sauerkraut, rinsed and drained
2 medium apples, cut into thin wedges
1 tablespoon chopped pimiento
1 teaspoon caraway seed
4 fully cooked smoked pork loin rib chops, cut ½ inch thick (about 1 pound)

In a 10-inch skillet cook onion in the butter or margarine till tender but not brown. Add the drained sauerkraut, apple wedges, pimiento, caraway seed, and ½ cup *water.* Cover and simmer 5 minutes. Place the chops on top of the sauerkraut mixture. Cover and simmer about 10 minutes more or till chops are heated through. Serve the chops with the sauerkraut mixture. Makes 4 servings.

Black Bean Soup

Caribbean

1 pound dry black beans (about 2½ cups)
1 or 2 meaty ham bones *or* smoked pork hocks (about 1 pound)
1 cup chopped onion
2 cloves garlic, minced
2 bay leaves
½ teaspoon salt
¼ teaspoon pepper
1 tablespoon vinegar

Rinse beans. Place in a large kettle with enough cold water to cover. Bring to boiling; reduce heat and simmer 2 minutes. Remove from heat; cover and let stand 1 hour. Drain beans, discarding liquid. Add the ham bone or pork hocks, onion, garlic, bay leaves, salt, pepper, and 7 cups *water.* Bring to boiling; reduce heat. Simmer, covered, for 2 to 2½ hours or till beans are very tender. Remove ham bone or pork hocks; when cool enough to handle, cut meat off bone and dice meat. Discard bone. Remove and discard bay leaves. Place 2 *cups* of the bean mixture in blender container; cover and blend till smooth. Return to soup with diced meat and the vinegar. Season to taste with additional salt and pepper. Heat through. Makes 4 servings.

Pork Enchiladas

Mexico

1 16-ounce can tomatoes
1 8-ounce can tomato sauce
1 4-ounce can green chili peppers, rinsed and seeded
1 small green pepper, cut up
1 clove garlic
½ teaspoon coriander seed
¼ teaspoon salt

2 cups finely chopped cooked pork
¾ cup shredded Monterey Jack *or* cheddar cheese (3 ounces)
¼ cup finely chopped onion
¼ teaspoon salt
2 tablespoons cooking oil
12 6-inch flour tortillas
1 cup shredded Monterey Jack *or* cheddar cheese (4 ounces)

In a blender container combine the *undrained* tomatoes, tomato sauce, chili peppers, green pepper, garlic, coriander, and ¼ teaspoon salt. Cover; blend just till smooth. Set aside.

Combine the cooked pork, ¾ cup Monterey Jack or cheddar cheese, the onion, and ¼ teaspoon salt. Set the mixture aside.

In a skillet heat the cooking oil. Dip tortillas, one at a time, into hot oil for 10 seconds or just till limp. Drain on paper toweling. Spoon pork mixture on tortillas; roll up. Place seam side down in a 13x9x2-inch baking dish. Pour tomato mixture atop. Cover with foil. Bake in a 350° oven about 30 minutes or till heated through. Remove the foil. Sprinkle the 1 cup shredded Monterey Jack or cheddar cheese atop. Return to oven for about 5 minutes or till cheese melts. Makes 6 servings.

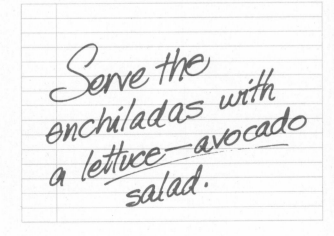

Serve the enchiladas with a lettuce—avocado salad.

Chicken and Fruit

Mexico

4 ounces chorizo or Italian sausage link, sliced
1 3-pound broiler-fryer chicken, cut up
2 slices fresh pineapple, cut ½ inch thick or one 8-ounce can pineapple slices (juice pack)

---

1 7½-ounce can tomatoes, cut up
1 cup chicken broth
1 medium onion, cut up
3 tablespoons blanched almonds
1 clove garlic
2 teaspoons sugar
1 teaspoon crushed red pepper*
⅛ teaspoon ground cinnamon

---

2 tart cooking apples, peeled and sliced
1 cup frozen peas
1 green-tipped banana, sliced
1 tablespoon lemon or lime juice

Brown the sausage in a 4-quart Dutch oven. Remove the sausage, reserving the drippings in the Dutch oven. Brown chicken pieces in the drippings. Return sausage to the Dutch oven. Place the pineapple slices atop the chicken. (Drain canned pineapple slices, reserving the pineapple juice for another use.)

In blender container combine the *undrained* tomatoes, chicken broth, onion, almonds, garlic, sugar, crushed red pepper,* and cinnamon. Cover and blend till smooth. Pour over the chicken and chorizo in Dutch oven. Cover and simmer 30 minutes. Add the apple slices and peas; cover and simmer about 10 minutes more. Stir in the banana slices and lemon or lime juice just before serving. Makes 6 to 8 servings.

*Or, substitute 2 dried ancho chilies and 2 dried pasilla chilies for the 1 teaspoon crushed red pepper. To prepare the dried chilies, cut them open. Discard stems and seeds. Cut chilies into small pieces using scissors or a knife. Place in a bowl; cover with boiling water. Let stand 1 hour; drain. Add the drained peppers to blender container in place of the crushed red pepper.

Tostadas

Mexico

2 cups dry pinto beans
6 cups cold water
6 cups hot water
½ cup chopped onion
1 teaspoon salt
1 8-ounce can tomato sauce
1 4-ounce can green chili peppers, rinsed, seeded, and chopped
1 teaspoon chili powder
1 teaspoon sugar
¼ teaspoon garlic powder

---

8 tostada shells
2 cups shredded cheddar cheese (8 ounces)
2 cups shredded lettuce
1 medium tomato, chopped
1 medium avocado, halved, seeded, peeled, and chopped
Taco sauce, dairy sour cream, or plain yogurt (optional)

Rinse pinto beans; add the 6 cups cold water. Bring to boiling; reduce heat and simmer 2 minutes. Remove from heat; cover. Let stand 1 hour. (Or, add beans to the 6 cups cold water and soak overnight.) Drain.

In large saucepan combine drained beans, the 6 cups hot water, the onion, and salt. Bring to boiling. Reduce heat; simmer, covered, about 2 hours or till beans are tender. Drain, reserving ½ cup cooking liquid. Mash beans slightly.

In a 10-inch skillet combine beans, reserved ½ cup liquid, tomato sauce, chili peppers, chili powder, sugar, and garlic powder. Bring to boiling; reduce heat. Simmer about 10 minutes, stirring the mixture occasionally.

Arrange tostada shells on a baking sheet. Heat in a 250° oven about 5 minutes or till warm. Top each tostada shell with bean mixture, cheddar cheese, shredded lettuce, tomato, and avocado. Pass taco sauce, sour cream, or yogurt, if desired. Makes 8 servings.

Sukiyaki

Japan

½ **pound beef sirloin steak**
3 **tablespoons sake** *or* **chicken broth**
3 **tablespoons soy sauce**
1 **teaspoon sugar**
2 **tablespoons cooking oil**
4 **ounces Chinese cabbage, cut into 1-inch**
   pieces (1¾ cups)
8 **green onions, bias sliced into 1-inch**
   lengths (1 cup)
1 **cup canned shirataki, drained (optional)**
½ **cup sliced fresh mushrooms**
½ **of an 8-ounce can bamboo shoots,**
   drained (½ cup)
4 **ounces fresh spinach, cut into 1-inch**
   strips (3 cups)
8 **ounces tofu (soybean curd), cut into**
   ¾-inch cubes

Partially freeze beef. Slice beef very thinly across the grain into bite-size strips; set aside. Combine the sake or broth, soy sauce, and sugar; set aside. Preheat a wok or a 10-inch skillet over high heat; add oil. Add the beef to hot wok; stir-fry 2 minutes or till meat is just browned. Add Chinese cabbage, onions, shirataki if desired, mushrooms, and bamboo shoots. Stir the soy mixture; stir into vegetable mixture. Cook and stir till bubbly. Stir in the spinach and tofu. Cover and cook for 1 to 2 minutes or just till ingredients are heated through and spinach is wilted. Makes 3 or 4 servings.

← *Shirataki, available in cans, is made from the starch of a Japanese root plant.*

Stir-Fried Chicken and Vegetables

China

1½ **pounds whole chicken breasts, skinned, halved lengthwise, and boned**
½ **cup cold water**
3 **tablespoons soy sauce**
1 **tablespoon cornstarch**
2 **tablespoons dry sherry**
1 **teaspoon grated gingerroot**

2 **tablespoons cooking oil**
4 **green onions, bias sliced into 1-inch lengths**
8 **ounces fresh mushrooms (3 cups), sliced**
½ **of an 8-ounce can bamboo shoots, drained (½ cup)**
½ **cup broken walnuts**
1 **cup frozen peas, thawed**

Cut chicken into 1-inch pieces. Set aside. In small bowl combine water, soy sauce, and cornstarch; stir in the dry sherry and gingerroot.

Preheat a wok or large skillet over high heat; add cooking oil. Stir-fry the green onions in hot oil 2 minutes or till crisp-tender. Remove from wok. Add the mushrooms and bamboo shoots; stir-fry 1 to 2 minutes. Remove from wok. Add walnuts to wok; stir-fry 1 to 2 minutes or till just golden, adding more oil if necessary. Remove walnuts. Add *half* of the chicken to hot wok or skillet; stir-fry 2 minutes. Remove from wok. Stir-fry remaining chicken 2 minutes. Return all chicken to wok or skillet. Stir soy mixture; stir into chicken. Cook and stir till thickened and bubbly. Stir in the onions, mushrooms, bamboo shoots, walnuts, and peas. Cover and cook 1 minute more. Serve at once. Makes 4 to 6 servings.

Lamb Curry

India

1½ **pounds boneless lamb, cut into 1-inch cubes**
2 **tablespoons cooking oil *or* peanut oil**
2 **medium onions, chopped**
1 **clove garlic, minced**
1 **tablespoon curry powder**
½ **teaspoon ground ginger**
Dash ground cinnamon
1 **16-ounce can tomatoes, cut up**
¾ **cup water**
¾ **teaspoon salt**
2 **medium potatoes, peeled and cut into 1-inch pieces**
1 **medium green pepper, cut into strips**
⅓ **cup cold water**
3 **tablespoons all-purpose flour**

In a 10-inch skillet brown *half* the lamb cubes at a time in the hot oil. Remove meat from skillet and set aside. Add onions, garlic, curry powder, ginger, and cinnamon; cook till onion is tender and lightly browned. Return meat to skillet along with the *undrained* tomatoes, ¾ cup water, and salt. Cover and simmer for 1 hour. Add the potatoes and green pepper. Cover and simmer 30 minutes more. Combine ⅓ cup cold water and flour. Stir into lamb mixture; cook and stir till thickened and bubbly. Cook and stir 1 to 2 minutes more. Serves 6.

Wok Care

Season a new wok before using. First scrub wok with cleanser or scouring pads to remove the rust-resistant coating applied during manufacturing. Wipe wok; heat on range to dry. Heat 2 tablespoons cooking oil in pan; tilt and rotate wok till entire inner surface is coated. Cool; dry with paper toweling.

After each use, soak wok in hot water. Use a bamboo brush or a sponge to clean it. Rinse, hand dry, and heat wok on range to dry excess water. Rub 1 teaspoon cooking oil over inner surface.

Hungarian Steak

Hungary

1½ pounds beef round steak, cut into
    6 pieces
1 teaspoon salt
⅛ teaspoon pepper
2 tablespoons cooking oil
½ cup chopped onion
1 cup beef broth
½ teaspoon sugar
½ teaspoon finely shredded lemon peel
¼ teaspoon dry mustard
1 bay leaf

5 carrots, cut into julienne strips
3 stalks celery, sliced
1 medium onion, sliced
1 tablespoon lemon juice
1 teaspoon drained capers
1 cup dairy sour cream
2 tablespoons all-purpose flour

Sprinkle meat with the salt and pepper. In a 12-inch skillet brown meat on both sides in hot oil. Add ½ cup chopped onion and cook till onion is tender. Add beef broth, sugar, lemon peel, dry mustard, and bay leaf. Cover; simmer 30 minutes. Add carrot strips, celery slices, onion slices, lemon juice, and the drained capers. Bring to boiling. Reduce heat and simmer, covered, 15 minutes more or till vegetables are tender. Remove bay leaf. Combine sour cream and flour. Stir into skillet mixture. Cook and stir till mixture is thickened and bubbly. Makes 6 servings.

Another time try the steak recipe with pork shoulder blade steaks (or) lamb shoulder blade chops.

Goulash

Hungary

1 pound boneless pork or beef stew meat,
    cut into 1-inch cubes
¼ cup chopped onion
1 clove garlic, minced
1 tablespoon lard or cooking oil
1 teaspoon paprika
1 16-ounce can sauerkraut, drained and
    snipped
½ teaspoon caraway seed
¾ cup dairy sour cream
1 tablespoon all-purpose flour

In 10'inch skillet cook meat, onion, and garlic in lard or cooking oil till meat is brown. Sprinkle with paprika, ¼ teaspoon *salt,* and ¼ teaspoon *pepper.* Add ¾ cup *water.* Cover and simmer 45 minutes. Add the sauerkraut and caraway seed. Cover and simmer about 15 minutes more. Combine the sour cream and flour. Stir into mixture in skillet. Cover; heat through. *Do not boil.* Serves 4.

Paella

Spain

1 2½- to 3-pound broiler-fryer chicken,
    cut up
1 teaspoon salt
2 tablespoons olive oil or cooking oil
1 cup cubed fully cooked ham
1 medium onion, chopped (½ cup)
1 tomato, peeled and chopped
1 clove garlic, minced
1½ cups chicken broth
1 cup long grain rice
¼ teaspoon thread saffron, crushed
½ pound fresh or frozen shelled shrimp
1 cup fresh or frozen peas

Sprinkle chicken pieces with the salt. In 12-inch skillet or paella pan brown chicken slowly in hot oil for 5 to 10 minutes, turning chicken occasionally. Drain off fat. Add ham, onion, tomato, and garlic. Stir in chicken broth, *uncooked* rice, and saffron. Bring mixture to boiling. Reduce heat. Cover and simmer 20 minutes. Add shrimp and peas. Bring to boiling. Reduce heat and simmer, covered, 5 minutes more or till rice, shrimp, and vegetables are done. Serves 8.

White Lamb Stew

Ireland

1 pound boneless lamb, cut into ¾-inch cubes
1 medium onion, cut into thin wedges
1½ teaspoons salt
¼ teaspoon pepper
2 large potatoes, peeled and sliced
2 carrots, sliced
1 medium turnip, peeled and chopped
1 tablespoon snipped parsley
¼ teaspoon dried thyme, crushed
2 to 3 tablespoons all-purpose flour

In Dutch oven combine the lamb, onion, salt, pepper, and 3½ cups *water.* Bring to boiling. Reduce heat; cover and simmer 40 minutes. Stir in potatoes, carrots, turnip, parsley, and thyme. Cover; cook 20 minutes more or till vegetables are tender. Combine flour and ½ cup *cold water.* Add to meat-vegetable mixture. Cook and stir till thickened and bubbly. Cook and stir 1 minute more. Season with salt and pepper, if desired. Serves 4.

Spiced Beef and Onion Stew

Greece

1 pound beef stew meat, cut into 1-inch cubes
2 tablespoons olive oil *or* cooking oil
1 clove garlic, minced
1 bay leaf
½ teaspoon ground cinnamon
3 whole cloves
1 8-ounce can tomato sauce
2 tablespoons vinegar
2 cups frozen small whole onions (½ of a 20-ounce package)
⅓ cup raisins

In a large saucepan brown meat, half at a time, in hot oil. Return all meat to pan. Stir in the garlic, bay leaf, cinnamon, cloves, and 1 teaspoon *salt.* Add tomato sauce, vinegar, and 1 cup *water.* Bring to boiling. Reduce heat. Cover and simmer 1 hour or till meat is nearly tender. Add onions and raisins. Bring to boiling; reduce heat. Cover; simmer 30 minutes more or till meat and onions are tender. Remove and discard bay leaf and cloves before serving. Makes 4 servings.

Moussaka

Greece

1 medium eggplant (1 pound), peeled and cut into ½-inch thick slices
Cooking oil *or* olive oil
1 pound ground lamb
½ cup chopped onion
1 clove garlic, minced
1 8-ounce can tomato sauce
2 tablespoons snipped parsley
½ teaspoon salt
¼ teaspoon ground cinnamon
1 bay leaf

2 tablespoons butter *or* margarine
2 tablespoons all-purpose flour
¼ teaspoon salt
Dash pepper
1½ cups milk
1 beaten egg
3 tablespoons grated romano *or* Parmesan cheese
1 tablespoon snipped parsley

Brush eggplant slices lightly with oil. Place on rack of broiler pan. Broil 3 to 4 inches from heat about 5 minutes on each side, or till browned. Place *half* the eggplant slices in the bottom of an 8x8x2-inch baking dish; set aside.

Meanwhile, in a 10-inch skillet cook lamb, onion, and garlic till meat is browned; drain off excess fat. Stir in the tomato sauce, the 2 tablespoons parsley, ½ teaspoon salt, cinnamon, and bay leaf. Bring to boiling. Reduce heat and simmer, covered, 10 minutes. Remove the bay leaf.

In saucepan melt the butter or margarine; stir in the flour, ¼ teaspoon salt, and the pepper. Add milk all at once. Cook and stir till mixture is thickened and bubbly. Slowly stir *half* of the hot mixture into the beaten egg; return all to saucepan. Cook and stir over low heat 2 minutes. Stir in 2 *tablespoons* of the grated cheese. Set aside. Spoon all of the meat mixture over eggplant layer in baking dish. Arrange remaining eggplant atop. Pour the milk-egg sauce over all. Sprinkle with remaining 1 tablespoon cheese. Bake, uncovered, in a 350° oven about 30 minutes or till set. Sprinkle top with the 1 tablespoon parsley. Let stand 10 minutes before cutting into squares. Makes 4 servings.

Bouillabaisse

France

10 clams in shells
2 pounds fresh *or* frozen fish fillets (a combination of any two or more such as sole, haddock, whiting, perch, red snapper, cod, *or* bass)
2 6-ounce fresh *or* frozen lobster tails
4 ripe tomatoes, peeled and chopped *or* two 16-ounce cans tomato wedges
2 medium onions, chopped (1 cup)
2 tablespoons snipped parsley
2 cloves garlic, minced
3 tablespoons olive oil *or* cooking oil
1 teaspoon instant chicken bouillon granules
1 teaspoon dried thyme, crushed
2 bay leaves
¼ teaspoon thread saffron
¼ teaspoon fennel seed, crushed
3 cups water
1 cup dry white wine
2 tablespoons tomato paste

Cover clams with salt water, let stand 15 minutes. (Use ⅓ cup salt to 1 gallon water for soaking.) Rinse. Repeat soaking twice more; drain.

Thaw fish and lobster, if frozen. When lobster is partially thawed, cut crosswise to make 8 portions. Cut fish into 1½-inch pieces.

In Dutch oven cook fresh tomatoes*, onions, parsley, and garlic in oil about 5 minutes or till onion is tender. Add bouillon granules, thyme, bay leaves, saffron, fennel, ½ teaspoon *salt,* and ¼ teaspoon *pepper.* Stir in the 3 cups water, the wine, and the tomato paste. Heat to boiling. Add fish, lobster, and clams; return to boiling. Reduce heat and simmer, covered, 6 to 8 minutes or till clams are open and fish is done. Season to taste with additional salt and pepper. Discard bay leaves. Serve with sliced French bread, if desired. Makes 8 servings.

*If using canned tomatoes, add the *undrained* tomato wedges with the water, white wine, and tomato paste.

Onion Quiche

France

1¼ cups all-purpose flour
½ teaspoon salt
⅓ cup shortening
3 to 4 tablespoons cold water

2 medium onions, sliced
2 tablespoons water
3 beaten eggs
1½ cups light cream *or* milk
1 tablespoon all-purpose flour
¼ teaspoon salt
¼ teaspoon ground nutmeg
Dash pepper
2 cups shredded Swiss *or* Gruyère cheese
(8 ounces)

In mixing bowl stir together the 1¼ cups flour and ½ teaspoon salt. Cut in the shortening, using a pastry blender till pieces are the size of small peas. Using the cold water, sprinkle 1 tablespoon over part of the mixture; gently toss with a fork. Push to side of bowl. Repeat till all is moistened. Form dough into a ball. On floured surface roll out pastry till about ⅛ inch thick. Line a 9-inch pie plate or quiche dish. Trim pastry to ½ inch beyond edge. Flute edge of pastry high. Line pastry with double thickness heavy-duty foil; fill with dry beans. Bake in a 450° oven for 5 minutes. Remove from oven; reduce oven temperature to 325°. Remove foil and dry beans. (Pastry shell should be hot when filling is added; do not partially bake shell ahead of time.)

In skillet or saucepan cook the onion slices, covered, in the 2 tablespoons water for 5 to 10 minutes or till onion is tender; drain well. Combine the eggs, cream or milk, 1 tablespoon flour, ¼ teaspoon salt, nutmeg, and pepper, using a wire whisk. Add the cooked onions and the cheese.

Place hot pastry shell on oven rack; pour egg mixture into shell. If necessary, cover edge of shell with foil to prevent overbrowning. Bake in a 325° oven for 30 to 35 minutes or till a knife inserted near center comes out clean. Let stand 10 minutes before serving. To serve, cut into wedges. Makes 6 servings.

This beef stew is elegant enough to serve to guests. Accompany with crusty French bread or rolls.

Beef Bourguignonne

France

2 pounds beef stew meat, cut into 1-inch cubes
3 tablespoons all-purpose flour
3 tablespoons butter *or* margarine
1 cup burgundy
1 cup beef broth
2 medium carrots, sliced
2 stalks celery, sliced
1 tablespoon tomato paste
1 clove garlic, crushed
1 bay leaf
½ teaspoon dried thyme, crushed

2 slices bacon, cut into small pieces
1 pound small boiling onions *or* frozen small whole onions
½ pound fresh mushrooms, sliced
2 tablespoons butter *or* margarine
2 tablespoons snipped parsley

Toss beef cubes with the flour. In a 4-quart Dutch oven brown the beef cubes, half at a time, on all sides in the 3 tablespoons butter or margarine. Return all meat to pan. Add the burgundy, beef broth, carrots, celery, tomato paste, garlic, bay leaf, and thyme. Cover and bake in a 325° oven for 1¾ hours.

In a skillet cook and stir the bacon and small onions till bacon is crisp and onions are lightly browned; discard excess fat. Add to beef mixture and continue baking, covered, 30 minutes more.

In same skillet cook the mushrooms in the 2 tablespoons butter or margarine 4 to 5 minutes or till tender. Just before serving, stir the mushrooms and parsley into the beef mixture. Season to taste with pepper. Makes 8 servings.

Kedgeree

England

92

2 tablespoons butter *or* margarine
¼ teaspoon curry powder
1½ cups cooked rice
1 cup flaked, cooked fish (8 ounces)
2 hard-cooked eggs, chopped
2 tablespoons snipped parsley
¼ teaspoon salt
   Dash pepper
   Lemon wedges

In small skillet melt butter or margarine. Add curry powder; stir over low heat for 30 seconds. Stir in the cooked rice, cooked fish, chopped hard-cooked eggs, parsley, salt, and pepper. Cover and cook, stirring carefully once or twice, till heated through. Serve fish mixture with lemon wedges. Makes 2 servings.

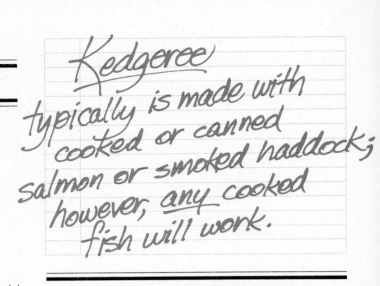

Kedgeree typically is made with cooked or canned salmon or smoked haddock; however, *any* cooked fish will work.

Seafood Salad

Scandinavia

6 cups torn lettuce (1 medium head)
1 8-ounce can whole oysters, drained
1 6-ounce package frozen cooked shrimp, thawed
1 5-ounce can lobster, drained, broken into large pieces, and cartilage removed
2 cups sliced fresh mushrooms (5 ounces)
½ cup sliced celery

½ cup salad oil
½ cup vinegar
2 teaspoons dried dillweed
¾ teaspoon sugar
¾ teaspoon salt
½ teaspoon prepared horseradish
3 medium tomatoes, cut into wedges
1 lemon, cut into 8 wedges

In a large salad bowl toss together the lettuce, drained oysters, shrimp, lobster pieces, sliced mushrooms, and celery. In screw-top jar combine the salad oil, vinegar, dillweed, sugar, salt, and horseradish. Cover and shake well.

Pour oil mixture over lettuce-seafood mixture. Toss to coat well. Add the tomato wedges and toss gently. Garnish each serving with a lemon wedge. Makes 8 servings.

Cornish Beef Pasties

England
Pictured on page 4

2 cups all-purpose flour
1 teaspoon salt
⅔ cup shortening
5 to 6 tablespoons cold water

1 medium potato
1 pound beef round steak, cut into ¼-inch cubes
⅔ cup peeled turnip, carrot, *or* rutabaga cut into ¼-inch cubes
½ cup finely chopped onion
1 teaspoon salt
¼ teaspoon pepper
   Milk
1 tablespoon sesame seed
   Catsup (optional)

In large mixing bowl stir together the flour and the 1 teaspoon salt. With pastry blender cut in the shortening till mixture resembles coarse crumbs. Add cold water, a tablespoon at a time, to dry ingredients, tossing with fork to moisten. Form dough into a ball. Cover and chill 1 hour.

Meanwhile, peel and coarsely chop potato. Combine with beef, turnip, onion, the 1 teaspoon salt, and the pepper. Set aside.

Divide dough into 5 portions. On lightly floured surface roll out each portion to a 7-inch circle. Place about ⅔ cup filling to one side of each circle; bring opposite side of pastry over filling. Pinch edges to seal. Cut slits in pastry for escape of steam. Brush pastry lightly with milk and sprinkle with sesame seed. Carefully transfer pasties to an ungreased baking sheet. Bake in a 375° oven for 35 to 40 minutes or till golden brown. Serve with catsup, if desired. Makes 5.

Index

D-K

L-O

Tips & Information